A TIME FOR PEACE

a paradigm shift and practical guide

foreword by Ambassador Miguel Diaz

DR. PRESTON LINDSAY

J. P. Zenger Books

BUILDING BRIDGES INITIATIVE

The International Encounter for Peace Event at Loyola University Chicago

Pope Francis called upon the Roman Catholic Church, in its entirety, to undertake a global process of shared discernment. He called Catholics at all levels, and in all types of institutions and situations to participate in this process of walking together and learning from one another. Pope Francis called this process the Synod on Synodality (2021-2024). Inspired by this call of Pope Francis, four professors from Loyola University Chicago (Felipe Legarreta, Peter Jones, Michael Murphy and Miguel H. Díaz) launched the Building Bridges Initiative (BBI). This initiative has generated a student-centered and university-organized series of events. The International Encounter for Peace event at Loyola University Chicago on March 7, 2026 is part of the Building Bridges initiative, inviting students, faculty, and practitioners to gather for a day of peacebuilding in the synodal spirit. The main objective of this event is to bring together women and men of good will from all walks of life to explore, discuss, and propose interdisciplinary avenues on how to promote peace among peoples of the human family . In the spirit of this initiative, and what

Pope Leo XIV has Latin America at the Holy See characterized as a peace that is "unarmed and disarming," we offer in this little book of peace tangible ways of making peace and building bridges.

For more information see:

The Building Bridges Initiative
at Loyola University Chicago
https://www.luc.edu/buildingbridges/

Building Bridges
an initiative of
the Pontifical Commission for Latin America (PCAL)
https://www.buildingbridges.va/

A Time for Peace

Foreword

Ambassador Miguel Diaz

I accepted Preston's invitation to walk with him thorough the landscape of peacebuilding, for as he first tells us in this insightful book in which he invites us into conversation, "peace is best nurtured and communicated one on one, face to face, and heart to heart…Peace has a cadence."

Walking involves body movements which are intentional and directional. And in our conversations, I discovered that positive peace is also a dynamic and evolving process that invites us to accompany other persons by contextually, sensorially, and attentively listening to them more than speaking. Truly, as my friend Preston imagines, peace is like a garden needing "preparation and care to take root, and only then can it grow."

Before undertaking this journey, Preston cautioned me that roadblocks, dead ends, and detours would be expected in our pursuit of peacebuilding. Still, he assured me in undertaking this journey, I would learn much about its guideposts central to the real work of peacebuilding. Things like transformation, othering, silence, empty space, biophilia, light, green spaces, natural sounds, grief, and storytelling, to name but a few so richly articulated in this book.

As I journeyed through *A Time for Peace*, I kept thinking of my favorite story, *The Little Prince*. The story recounts conversations between an airplane pilot who crashes in the Sahara Desert and a Little Prince who hails from a small planet. The Little Prince took good care of his planet, especially falling in love with a mysterious rose. While journeying, the narrator of the story recounts various encounters and conversations of the Little Prince, which climax with recounting his visit to earth and finding a rose garden. The Little Prince is surprised and saddened to find other roses, thinking his rose was one of a kind. But in the garden, he meets a wise fox that reveals to him the secret to life: "One sees clearly only with the heart. Anything essential is invisible to the eyes…It's the time you spent on your rose that makes your rose so important."

I invite you to read this book and take time to walk with Preston on this peacebuilding journey. He will entice you to see with the eyes of your heart enlightened. You will encounter valuable lessons to become a more successful peacebuilder, empowering you to take the time to care for your neighbors in the cadence of peace.

Miguel H. Díaz, PhD
U.S. Ambassador to the Holy See, ret.
John Courtney Murray, SJ, University Chair in Public
    Service, Loyola University Chicago
Senior Fellow for Religion and Peacebuilding, Alliance for
    Peacebuilding, Washington, DC.

---

hi

---

an introduction

Well hello, there.

Welcome to this little book about nurturing and curating peace. As you will soon see, the path of peace can be a fraught one, with twists and turns as we navigate our own internal dialogues and enculturations. I will do my very best here to make this a gentle journey moving forward as we navigate this sea of could of's, should haves, and other general strivings. Nevertheless, all of this considered, we'll find our way. As you will also see over the next few pages, at first glance peace can seem to be a very simple idea. Upon further inspection, however, it also comes with a loaded and often plodding complexity. This is true in the sense that it can be quite easy to say we want peace, and quite another thing to go about the work of applying the principles and techniques peace asks of us. I suppose like all really meaningful things, this should come as no surprise.

Also, as I'm sure you're aware by now, this book will be a conversation between the two of us. In my work and in my studies of peace, I have found that peace is best nurtured and communicated one on one, face to face, and heart to heart. As we so often say in our Peace Council group, "Peace has a cadence."

So from the very start, together we will walk alongside each other in patience, with open minds and hearts. In this, I will do my very best to help you feel taken care of in this respect. And hopefully, this book will feel like a warm drink, in front of a fireplace, wrapped in your favorite blanket.

However, we should first note a few markers on our path: one, the purpose of this book, like most knowledge in my opinion, is to be used. Two, in this space words matter. So we will take care to gently explore and build with them as we grow our understanding. And three, there is no magic cure, no hero to come save us, and absolutely no path before us that can cure every problem in the world.

There just isn't.

This may be the case because building peace is a naturally slow process. Peace simply takes time. It takes time as the foundation of peace lays in trust, and trust and connection only grow over time. Peace is much like a garden in this respect. It needs to have the necessary preparation and care to take root, and only then can it grow. And generally speaking, peacebuilders match this same cadence more often than not in ways that mirror the gentle garden; with a soft spoken nudge and an often shy demeanor.

So in this quiet culture of peace, we will allow the time and space for our own understanding and kinship to grow.

Our conversation over the following pages will be a rather straightforward one. In the first chapter, or as I like to think of it, a discussion, we will talk about what peace is; our second conversation will be on cultures of peace; our third diversion will be about spatial peace, and the tangible ways it impacts our lives; the fourth discussion will revolve around grief and sorrow; and the fifth will delve into how to connect with and understand the people around us, offering a few simple ways we can help people feel seen and heard. In this section, I will offer a few more practical ways to help us gently draw out the very best in ourselves, and those around us.

So in renewed kinship, let's explore and discuss some of the ways we can connect more deeply with our families, with our friends, and with our communities.

Chapter 1

on peace

MOST FOLKS BELIEVE peace is just the absence of war, or the absence of the threat of violence.

Peace is so much more than that, though.

Peace, or more accurately, positive peace, is what scholars, a few activists, some practitioners, and even a couple legislators rally around when discussions of peace do happen to occur. Although, even among these groups there is still a lot of confusion around what peace in actuality means.

. . .

Some of this lack of awareness, or what Paul Chappell refers to as peace illiteracy, is due to the quiet nature of most peacebuilders we touched on before. When engaging in the cultures and practices and ways of peace, these leave imprints on those nurturing it. In fact, it is near impossible to build and nurture peace without it having a lasting and transformative effect on us. As a result, peacebuilders tend to be quiet by nature, and not prone to engage in marketing campaigns or talk about all the good things they are a part of.

Because of this peacebuilder meekness, and the subsequent lack of peace literacy, it may be helpful for us to take a closer look at what the layers and levels of peace are.

WAR/SYSTEMIC DIRECT VIOLENCE

This section should come as no surprise. War is the governmental or organizational engagement in direct violence with another people, organization, culture, nation-state, or region. It is structural. It is cultural. And it is tragic. War is harmful for many reasons. The first being its effect on the people in it. One of the deeply sad realities of war is the fact that those most in danger aren't actually the soldiers. The vast majority of people who lose their lives, or are displaced in war, are women and children— who are rarely involved in the conflict itself. In fact, the safest place to be when a war starts is in the military.

Go figure.

In most instances the first sign that a people are on a path toward war is when othering is on the rise.

What is othering you ask?

Othering is to view or treat someone, or some people, as inherently different or alien to ourselves. Put plainly, othering is whoever you or I consider to be a "them," an out-group, the not like us, an untouchable. This is one of the first steps to war, violence, and frankly, to genocide: the othering. Then comes the distrust, the division, and eventually, the de-humanization.

NEGATIVE PEACE

This can be the most easy to understand, and the most familiar of the peace states. In the social state of negative peace, there isn't exactly a war going on, per sé. But there are consistent and recurring structural and cultural violence occurring against persons in a region, often beneath the surface through subtle forms of othering. There are also still a smattering of pockets of direct violence as well.

For example, this can look like when we move to a city and someone tells us to stay away from a certain part of the city as they believe it isn't safe, or there may be a food desert, or a food swamp there for that matter. When conducting preliminary research last year, I found that those same areas that struggle with direct violence and food deserts also happen to be the same areas that can struggle with connectivity and access to nature. These areas can then become a self-fulfilling cycle of systemic violence moving downward in descending negative cascades.

The ugly truth of it all is that these are social patterns. Nothing in our society just happens. These outcomes are the result of the social models and incentive structures of a region: a politics, a culture, an economy, and the spaces and places people wander in and around.

This is negative peace.

LIMINAL PEACE

This phase, or state, of peace can be a tumultuous one. By its name, we can see this phase is a transitory one. As a result, this is a process that is caught in the in-between. Liminal peace has many of the residual conflicts and violence leftover from negative peace. In this state people are beginning to gain more awareness of things while also looking toward to the future and imagining what things could be like.

This phase usually looks like knowledge sharing, or even reconciliation processes. There are often still unresolved divides—with anger, resentments, and deep traumas—but people are starting the difficult process of seeking to understand one another and transition their city, their neighborhood, and their relationships to ones that build trust, and help folks feel seen and taken care of.

Direct
Physical
Peace
Structural
Institutional
Peace
Cultural
Peace

POSITIVE PEACE

This state of peace is where the magic happens. Positive peace is the place where we see the coming together of cultures, of ideas, of weathered histories, all for the possibility of a more connected and trusting tomorrow.

Johann Galtung, the father of the peace and conflict studies field (PACS), discovered the concept after a few years of studying peace and conflict from a thorough mathematical perspective. That was his original background, after all, and he brought all the methods, praxis, and rigor to bear for it. Before Galtung, many people held the mistaken idea of a societal progression from war to peace. Galtung introduced the better theory that peace exists within a framework of complex systems, rather than on a supposed continuum. He proposed three main areas of focus that would contain all other systems of violence or peace within them. The first area is **structural** violence or peace. The second is **cultural** violence or peace. And the third is **direct** violence or peace.

Even more important than the three ways of understanding violence and peace that Galtung discovered, are the very fundamental natures of the systems at play.

For example, when I speak with people here or there about peace, as a concept it can be rather complex and difficult to understand at first. Until, that is, when I start sharing how that works in the real world, it often all comes together for folks.

Put simply, peace is our systems at work for our good. It is the how and the why of our interactions. One way to understand the interconnected nature of peace is to think of a forest. In order for this ecosystem to be healthy, tens of thousands of factors within the relationships of the flora and fauna need to be in balance. These are deep relationships that have evolved over time between the trees, the mushrooms, the fungal networks, and the birds and other crawling creatures. Each of these alone can impact how well the ecosystem fares one way or another.

We are the same. Our relationships matter. When our relationships are respected and nurtured, the result can be a healthy ecosystem. The result can be positive peace.

DISCUSSION

1. In what ways has negative peace influenced your life?
2. Has your community recognized the deep harms of structural violence?
3. In what ways have you seen elements of liminal, or positive peace?

ACTION

1. Organize and lead a discussion group with family and/or friends talking about what peace is.
2. Host a workshop on Peace Ecosystems in your neighborhood.
3. Submit a request in your next city council meeting to have your city express its desire to be recognized as a city of peace.

Chapter 2

cultures of peace

All right, the last chapter was a little thick with Peace and Conflict Studies jargon, so I'll try to boil it down a bit more in this one. After all, what is the point of a peace that doesn't make sense to people, that doesn't help us see where that path leads, and that doesn't give us tangible steps to help us get there?

So, we know that peace is rooted in our systems. We know that how those systems work are either for our benefit, or they're not. We also now know that due to peace and conflict being rooted in our systems, that means there are ways to influence the outcomes within those ecosystems.

This discussion will revolve around our social interactions, and the building blocks that frame them.

Which brings us to cultures of peace. Cultures of peace are critical for positive peace to take root. They are embedded in our values, attitudes, and behaviors when we nurture them. To understand cultures of peace, we must understand their foundation. The foundations of cultures of peace are:

- Non-Violence
- Interconnection
- Silence

Now some of you may be wondering about that last one, thinking to yourselves, "Why in the world is silence listed in here?" But hear me out. We'll get there.

NON-VIOLENCE

Non-violence first came into the public zeitgeist during the campaigns and non-violent civil uprisings led by Mahatma Gandhi at the turn of the 20th century. Non-violence is both a belief, and a way of living one's life, that seeks peaceful conflict resolution of events while also struggling for social justice without using physical violence in any form. As one would imagine, the theory and practice of this way of being is complex and involved, yet contains a heart of simplicity.

Gandhi actually had a book written on his teachings called, *Gandhi on Non-Violence*. Here's a short excerpt to help us understand non-violence a bit better.

> *Belief in non-violence is based on the assumption that human nature in its essence is one, and therefore unfailingly responds to the advances of love . . . The non-violent technique (its application) does not depend for its success on the goodwill of the dictators . . . a non-violent revolution is not a program of seizure of power. It is a program of transformation of relationships, ending in a peaceful transfer of power.*

Martin Luther King Jr. (MLK) and those engaged in the United States' Civil Rights movement also adhered to and used the principles of non-violence during their struggle. MLK was a staunch practitioner and advocate of non-violence, not just because it was the most effective path in conflict resolution, but because it is the moral way to address deep intergenerational conflict and oppressive imbalances of power. He said,

> *True pacifism, or nonviolent resistance, is a courageous confrontation of evil by the power of love. . . . The aftermath of nonviolence is the creation of the beloved community. The aftermath of nonviolence is redemption. The aftermath of nonviolence is reconciliation. The aftermath of violence is emptiness and bitterness.*

As we discussed in chapter one, the language of othering is the opposite of this. When we demean, slander, gossip, or undermine other people and their experience, it is not just damaging to them, this language and behavior undermines us as well. We cannot define someone else's behavior and worth without it having a cognitive and emotional effect on our own. Our brains and ways of relating to one another just don't work that way. In the same way, non-violence includes our words and our actions. It includes them both because the basis of non-violence and positive peace are the relationships that bind us all together. This leads us to our next discussion point, interconnection.

INTERCONNECTION

There are many traditions we can draw from here in order to understand what interconnection looks like in theory and practice. I suppose the first we can use as an example is what the Buddhist tradition calls interbeing. Interbeing is a key concept that comes out of Engaged Buddhism, in particular. The late Thich Nhat Hanh and his followers believe that interbeing means the understanding of the interdependence of all things. In their practice, they frequently use the example of a flower. They explain that it cannot exist first without the seed, then the soil, and the sun and rain and other elements of its environment. All of these parts make it a collective whole; each just as important as the next for the flower. All these elements contribute to its manifestation, to the conditions necessary for the very creation of the flower itself.

The next tradition that speaks to this is the Anishinaabe vision of connectedness, seen through the lens of right relationships, or treaties. The fundamental idea of these relationships are grounded in the seven grandfather teachings shared with the Ojibwe Nations. These are the teachings of wisdom, respect, love, honesty, humility, bravery, and truth. Each of these are not just seen as being in treaty with the other human brothers and sisters on Turtle Island (North America) but with all things within and on her. In other words they, of course, believe in the proper balance of relationships with their fellow humans, and also in their relationship and treaties with the earth and everything else in the environment as well.

The final example we'll use here is the Quaker tradition of interconnectedness. Much like the Buddhists and Anishinaabe, and even like the South African concept of Ubuntu, Quakers believe we exist as we are because of the relationships we have around us. They foster these relationships within and beyond their close-knit communities. They see the world as one large interconnected web of relationships in, or out of balance with one another. The Quakers also have a firm belief in the deep importance of silence.

SILENCE

Well, we made it. Silence isn't just a key component of cultures of peace for kicks and giggles. It is integral to both inner peace and systemic positive peace because it acts as the frame and default for our own listening.

We'll stick with the Quakers for a minute just to help illustrate the point. Many people aren't aware that Quakers meet each week in meetings all over the world not in a church house with a preacher at the front, but in a meeting for a shared hour of silence. Quakers believe that the divine speaks to us not from a pulpit, but from the silence. They would say that the New Testament calls this the Still Small Voice. And though I wouldn't consider myself a man of deep faith, I also don't disagree with them.

Flashes of insight and enlightenment consistently come for many people all over the world, with and without a faith tradition, while in deep contemplation, in pauses between conversations, in meditation, on quiet walks in nature, and while quietly working on this or that. These moments of silence ground the necessary ways of relating to one another with the space they need, by helping us to remember to give ourselves the space we need to connect with ourselves in silence.

Another example, and one of my favorite activities to use as an ice breaker for a workshop or class, is the one minute of silence activity. Silence, especially for folks in the West, can be a painful experience. We are enculturated (taught and trained from birth across society) to fill the empty space. In most of my experiences with folks, they have often found that silence can be quite difficult, even unsettling at first. Folks simply aren't used to letting the silence lengthen in conversation for 5, or 10, or even 30 seconds. Some people simply can't do it. For those that do endure, however, there is a light at the end of the tunnel.

People consistently report that the first 10 to 35 seconds are like static in their mind and body. In fact, it's so uncomfortable that they report feeling jittery and anxious. Like nails on a chalkboard. And then . . . . it's almost as if a weight is lifted, or a curtain is drawn back. Like we were discussing earlier, there is a letting go and a quietude, even an equanimity. After the initial discomfort, there is usually peace.

This points us toward another key aspect of silence: the open air it creates in dialogue. When we ourselves are quieting our minds and holding our tongues, folks report being better able to be present with those around them.

For instance, when was the last time you really listened to a stranger? Or to someone at work? Or even and especially with your own family? People need to feel heard in order to feel understood. Are we waiting to say what we want to say in a conversation, or are we listening to the words, the emotions, and the heart of the person in front of us? Connecting with others requires that we deeply listen to people and hear both what they're saying, and also what they're not.

It may sound simple, but saying you heard someone can make all the difference. It can be as easy as repeating back what you thought you heard, offering a smile, or even just nodding your head. One of the rarest things lately is for people to feel seen. We can help by just listening, by embracing the pregnant pauses . . . by being okay with the whispering silence. But more on that in chapter five.

INFRASTRUCTURES & CULTURES OF PEACE

So we know we need to practice non-violence. We need to regularly ponder and see the interconnectedness of all things, and we know how important it is to hold silence for ourselves and for others. These each lay the practical groundwork to understand and use cultures of peace. So now we move another step closer to a tangible practice of peace by discussing infrastructures and cultures of peace. In 2016 the United Nations released a report on infrastructures and cultures of peace (I4P). They did this so that governments, civil society groups, businesses, and educational institutions could understand more clearly how they could nurture and build more connected and peaceful societies.

At the time, I was living in Canada as I completed my doctoral studies in Peace and Conflict Studies (PACS). I had just completed my PhD candidate exams and when I read this report, it was huge for me. I felt the weight of its importance—it was like fireworks in my brain.

You see, PACS has had a bit of a struggle grounding the study, outcomes, and the social impacts of peacebuilding for a few decades. It has been hard for peacebuilders to know if their interventions are making a difference, for better or worse. The innovation of social impacts had yet to be applied to PACS. This was a gap that needed to be filled in order to make peace more tangible and accessible for people all over the world.

In 2017, my colleagues Sean Byrne, Ana Cristina De Figuierodo and I wrote a chapter that would later be called, *the ABC's of Measuring Positive Peace*. As with many book deals, this one was delayed, and was published as a chapter in the Palgrave Handbook of Positive Peace in 2023.

In the chapter we laid out 99 social impact measures across the areas of politics, culture, economics, and our urban environments. We did this to help people know how to understand the impacts of peace, and the gaps that exist in society with its absence. And in so doing we created a positive peace assessment. This step was important for many reasons, but mostly so peacebuilders, interested leaders, and grassroots communities on the ground can know where we are in regards to peace; so we can know if the work we're doing to nurture it is making a difference. So we conducted an extensive literature review of PACS and layered those findings over pre-existing social impact measures across the social and behavioral sciences, tethering the processes and outcomes of infrastructures and cultures of positive peace with social and environmental outcomes across society.

These peace measures aim to gauge the social flows of positive peace, so that people can create the peace they want, how they want; helping communities use the actual physical infrastructures of a city or region to make peace tangible; to make it usable.

For example, a few of these measures include connectivity, access to nature, and political voice. Connectivity is an indicator used in urban planning and design to measure how people can or can't move through their city, how often they see friends and family, feel like they can trust their neighbors, and if they feel like they can ask someone for help in a time of need or crisis.

Access to nature is pretty self-explanatory, but it really just means how close a person is to the natural environment in and around their homes and neighborhoods. It does this using addresses and zip/postal codes using satellite data and various other signifiers of nature proximity.

Political voice is quite the useful indictor used to measure how folks engage in their communities. It focuses on trust, institutional participation, and if they feel like they can make a difference in their community, among others. In some forms the indicator can include up to 19 different measures, but generally includes a half dozen or so.

These few measures, in just a short preamble, demonstrate important aspects of the deep interconnectedness of society. They also point us toward finding deeper ways of understanding each other. Infrastructures and and cultures of peace are vital to understanding this process, and of more intimately understanding positive peace. Those elements of non-violence, interconnection, and silence form their backbone. In one way or another these concepts influence the framing, the process, and the desired outcomes of positive peace.

In the discussion throughout this chapter we've outlined what cultures of peace are, what the three underlying currents that connect and frame them are, and we have expanded on cultures of peace by introducing infrastructures and cultures of peace, serving to further deepen the impacts of cultures of peace while also creating a social impact framework to measure them. All of this leads us to our next topic of discussion in this little book: spatial peace.

DISCUSSION TOPICS

1. How has non-violence affected your relationships today?
2. In what ways could you practice more non-violence in your relationships?
3. How might you help build infrastructures and cultures of peace in your city?

ACTION ITEMS

1. Listen to a family member without a thought of what you may say in response.
2. Take some time to be in silence today. After few minutes of quietude, what thoughts and impressions rise to the top?

Chapter 3

---

spatial peace

Well done.

I know we've touched on quite a few topics in our discussions here, and well done, you, for making it this far. We have a few to go yet, and you're just over halfway through.

Our discussion on spatial peace is so important because it really does touch each aspect of our lives every day. For example, the impacts of noise pollution on sleep and student learning, or the way natural light can decrease instances of conflict. Also, are there parks, walking paths, or food swamps in your neighborhood?

The ways in which we walk around or otherwise meander through our communities for this or that either help or hinder our own access to peace.

One of the sad parts of talking about spatial peace is due to the confusing history of peace itself; with it's fraught politics, and its often abused use as a term, the tangible and truly accessible aspects of peace can be lost to us in the mix. The word peace has been misused all over the world, too often as a weapon to tell people what they need, why their problems didn't matter, or that someone else held all the solutions to their worries, and they needed to pay for it. Perhaps no other field has seen so plainly the tragic effects of negative peace more than in the urban development, architecture, and in urban planning implementation teams. They have been devastating on communities. It doesn't have to be this way. And in fact, there are already many folks working to change this around the world.

We can talk about the efforts of folks to increase rates of walkability, connectivity, change zoning laws, or mixed use density, and on, but what these efforts are really pointing toward are the simple ways we can have what need around our homes. For example, how far away are family and friends from us? Do we need to drive to see see them for longer than 10 minutes? Or maybe, is there a grocery store within walking distance? How about a reliable and safe public transit? Or maybe even bicycle lanes that we see women and children using regularly? These may seem like small things at first, but when viewed in their place in the larger picture, they point to the basic needs of belonging and connection being met or not.

Peace and conflict have deep and lasting impacts on our lives every time we step out of our front doors, every time we walk around our neighborhoods, and every time we head to the store for groceries. There are a myriad of ways we can talk about spatial peace, so lets start with the most tangible first.

THE SENSES

It is important to note, before we move any further into how space and place influence our ability to connect with one another, that we are human. This may seem odd at first, and little too obvious. But think about it . . . When you enter into a room what do your eyes do? What is the temperature? Does the temperature make you want to grab a blanket or a cold drink? Are there people you like in the room? Is there natural light coming through the window, or are the lights fluorescent? And how is the air? Stale and stuffy, or cool with a slight breeze. Are there any plants in the room? And on. As can be clearly seen here, all of these have direct impacts on not only our perceptions, but in unconscious and often invisible ways. All of these things can be stacked and added upon for either our benefit and comfort, or for our discomfort and harm.

To say we are creatures of our environments is a bit of an understatement, and an oversimplification. For example, there are thousands of different perceptions running through our unconscious minds and bodies at any given point, everyday, all day. The sheer volume of the capacity required of our minds for this is staggering. Think for a moment about what you would consider to be a good day.

What does it look like?

What does it feel like?

How was your morning?

Is it smooth and fluid?

And what makes it that way?

What does your evening look like?

What does it feel like?

Are there candles, blankets, or a warm drink?

Maybe a bath?

These questions, when considering our sensory needs, carry a lot more weight to them. They also have a lot to do with our own cultural lenses. Demonstrating again just how complex and interwoven peace can be in our everyday lives.

Now how about your bad days.

We've all had them. The kind of days where there is just too much swirling inside us. The kind of days where we felt like an open and raw nerve. Where we may have been irritated, or sharp, or even lashed out.

Did we get angry with someone at work, or maybe a loved one? What was it that we reacted to?

The truth is we react to our physical environments mostly in our subconscious mind and body. In what social scientists and therapists refer to as our **cognitive loads**, or **windows of tolerance**, we are far too often pushing ourselves past our mental, emotional, and sensory limits. Particularly in the West.

When these pools of sensory and cultural cues are more soothed and balanced in our physical/spatial environments, however, we then mirror this balance in our minds and bodies. When we have space physically, we also have space mentally in the form of less subconscious stress. One fact that came as a surprise to me a few years back was the simple truth that most of our thoughts and impressions are unconscious, or non-conscious. Almost a full 90 percent of our perceptions are non-conscious. Which brings us to our next point of focus here: biophilia.

BIOPHILIA

Our DNA has been designed to react and move with our natural environments; to fit within an ecosystem tailored to and with our own basic physical and social needs. Biophilia is the draw to, and interdependence of a species with nature. As should come as no surprise, we are a biophilic species. Nature has deep and lasting impacts on us when we have access to it, and when we don't. Edward O. Wilson was the first person who studied this connection in depth, coining the very term of biophilia in 1984. He wrote,

We are human in good part because of the particular way we affiliate with other organisms. They are the matrix in which the human mind originated and is permanently rooted, and they offer the challenge and freedom innately sought. To the extent that each person can feel like a naturalist, the old excitement of the untrammeled world will be regained. I offer this as a formula of re-enchantment to invigorate poetry and myth: mysterious and little-known organisms live within walking distance of where you sit. Splendor awaits in minute proportions.

Humans are nature. We are not separate from it, but just a small part of its vast systems. This is a primary aspect of biophilia. Humans are drawn to nature, Wilson says, because we *are* nature. Study after study has come since he first spoke of it, and each has reaffirmed this simple fact. The positive effects of nature are deep within us, everyday. Access to nature, and the biophilic responses experienced in it, are vital to our overall well-being, health, and our potential to experience positive peace.

This is what we'll discuss for rest of this chapter. In this, to start us off we will highlight just three specific ways that space and place effect us: light, greenery, and sound.

LIGHT

Natural light has many mental, emotional, and general health benefits for us. Natural light helps us sleep better, and can even help with depression. Sarah Williams Goldhagen tells us,

> *Natural light, like pastoral views, heals the sick and improves well-being even of the well by affecting our cognitive processes in profound, although subtle ways. For example, hospital patients in rooms with natural light sleep better, feel less stress, feel less pain, and heal more quickly than those patients in rooms without natural light.*

Natural light can also effect the classroom. Children in classrooms with natural light perform better on tests, remember class topics better, have less behavior issues, and just generally have better focus in class when compared to students without it.

Access to natural light also reduces depression and dementia rates, while also decreasing the length of hospital patient stays.

GREEN SPACE

Studies have also found that green spaces act as protectors for our mental health. They also increase our attention, reduce stress, while decreasing the impacts of anxiety disorders, attention deficit, and hyperactive disorders. And, go figure, nature access also increases birth weight in newborns and helps protect against overall mortality.

Put simply, when communities have access to green spaces they are not only healthier, there is also less crime and less overall conflict within them. When there are accessible green spaces, communities simply feel more connected with one another. The effects of infrastructures of peace are felt deeply across the world. Access to natural light, green space, and other natural aspects make us happier, healthier, and less prone to conflict.

SOUND

Sound is the most visceral of the senses. It is found in nerve center of the fight/flight/freeze part of the brain. Because of this we react to sound often before we are conscious of our reaction. In fact, we don't even need to be aware of a sound in order for our spinal cord and non-conscious thoughts to adjust our relationship to its source.

We will forego the noise pollution aspects of the impacts of sound on our behaviors here, with the caveat that they are worse than we could imagine, literally costing lives and millions of folks sanity all around the world. Please see the references at the end of this little book if you'd prefer to witness the tragedy up close.

Alternatively, the impacts of silence or natural sounds, are equally profound, and what we'll discuss for the rest of the chapter.

In contrast to city-scape sounds, which can cause a fight-flight-freeze responses, natural sounds have the opposite effect. Pena tells us,

> *listening to existing noises in nature has incredibly positive effects, including a decrease in stress and pain, an improvement in cognitive performance, an enhancement in mood, and much more.*

When it comes to actual silence, or absence of noise pollution in any form, it has been found that it improves overall health by lowering blood pressure, improving concentration and focus, calming racing thoughts, stimulating brain growth, reducing cortisol levels, nurturing creativity, and helping insomnia, all while encouraging mindfulness (i.e. awareness of the self in the present moment). There is a laundry list of the benefits of silence on us. Silence could also provide a more tailored way forward in peacebuilding, possibly increasing the effectiveness of spatial peacebuilding strategies for healthier and more peaceful cities.

In this discussion we have talked about spatial peace, and in doing so, pointed toward our own biophilic natures, adding a little more to the already deep knowledge on infrastructures and cultures of peace discussed earlier. We have also learned about the effects of nature on our health, our behaviors, and our capacity to be with one another. After all, it's difficult to listen to one another if there is a semi-truck blaring its horn, or if we've been under fluorescent lights for 10 hours. There are spatial environments that help us, and there are spaces and places that hinder us—disturbing the cognitions that foster connection, trust, and belonging.

So before we attempt to engage with our loved ones, or maybe even a stranger who vehemently disagrees with us, we should consider the course of our own day, with their effects on our mental and emotional primers and cognitive loads. After this consideration, we should then consider the best possible places to engage constructively with our loved ones, or maybe even that stranger so bent on disagreeing with us.

DISCUSSION

1. How far are your family and friends away from you; in minutes and miles?
2. Do you frequently see women and children out and about in your city's public spaces?
3. How far do you need to travel for fresh bread or a community discussion?

ACTION ITEMS

1. Look around your home for a moment. Consider what rooms you feel more relaxed in, what rooms you may feel more anxious in. What small changes can be made to increase your peace?
2. Now look around your neighborhood. Are there trees/greenery, tended walkways, and enough lighting for you to feel safe walking at night?
3. Attend a City Council urban planning meeting. What is your community doing to increase walkability and make it easier for folks to connect with each other?

Chapter 4

----

holding grief

Hopefully by now this doesn't come as a surprise, but life is hard.

It can, and often does, flip us over and swing us about like a rag doll. It can tear out our hearts while simultaneously preparing to take our homes, our families, our minds, and even our sense of who we are. The tragedy of this suffering is that when we are in it, when we are caught in the throes of the dark place of grief, we often feel isolated and alone. Even when there are people all around us, we can still feel the hollowness there, the numb remove.

I know that in my first real season on grief, I felt this too. I was so broken, so irreversibly shattered, there was no going back to the before version of myself. He was gone. I broke, I broke again, and then again.

I know I'm not alone in this. Too many people experience this deep breaking. It's crushing. And far too many people don't have the support they need to pass through to the other side of it.

It can be so easy, too easy, to lash out in our trauma when the fracturing is fresh—to seek some form of revenge, even if only in some small way. There can be a deep sense of injustice and wrongness to the dark place . . . it can be overwhelming and confusing. And as history and healing have shown us, revenge doesn't lead us out of grief, it most often just deepens it. Because now we are also responsible for enacting violence, and the cycle continues.

This shared pain connects and binds us. And here is a little secret: pain and suffering opens up our hearts and leads us to dig within ourselves for the strength to build peace. After the dust has settled and we've taken measure of the sorrows all around us, we are what remain. And in our shared grief, we can build a better way.

How we help each other move in and through grief is vital for the processes of true connection and belonging. And for the deep work required for peace to take root. As Senegalese elders say, if one doesn't process the grief, it comes out in another, often more hurtful way in community.

Thich Nhat Hanh has said,

> *There is a way of getting in touch with suffering without being overwhelmed by it. We try to avoid suffering, but suffering [can be] useful. We need suffering. Going back to listen and understand our suffering brings about the birth of compassion and love. If we take the time to listen deeply to our own suffering, we will be able to understand it. Any suffering that has not been released and reconciled will continue. Until it has been understood and transformed, we carry with us not just our own suffering but also that of our parents and ancestors. Getting in touch with the suffering that has been passed down to us helps us understand our own suffering.*

SILENCE

So we return to the silence.

Think back and remember our discussion on cultures of peace. What does silence do? What does it create?

Silence creates space.

Most often when one of us is in the dregs of sorrow and grief we don't want anything, really. Other than what we may have lost, that is. What we want is time. Time to rest. Time to listen. Time to sit. Time away from the noise —especially social noise. And we want safety to be in our grief.

When we're in it, really in it, everything becomes so loud around us. It's all cacophonous and overwhelming. Loved ones may offer a smile or a helping hand in hope of our healing. Yet we remain tethered to our sorrow.

This is because when we suffer a loss, we lose not just the person or people or past, we lose the spaces and places we used to be in. The safety and security we felt there. And the connections we made in place. We grieve not just the initial loss itself, but also the parts of us that are now gone.

STORIES

One of the most helpful ways of processing grief and loss is through shared mediums where we can experience emotions in a safe way.

It is not uncommon for people to watch a favorite show a hundred times, or listen to music, or wander through old familiar books that won't throw us back into the dark.

All of this is storytelling.

Sharing in stories will often ask us to encounter some facet of our shared grief—both within others and ourselves. We can learn to navigate the pain, and help our people do the same by holding space to meander familiar paths in song, and in the written and spoken word.

When we approach the honor of hearing someone's story, we must not do so violently. Just listen, then affirm. And we must never offer platitudes, or silver linings. With grief, silence is better than speech nine times out of ten. Just be present with them, and with yourself.

Without seeing them as a whole person, with experiences that are valid no matter how uncomfortable, we will fail them. And we will fail each other in the process. If we cannot sit in shared sorrow, and if we do offer platitudes or ask them to move past it before they're ready, then we are not truly listening.

This can be uncomfortable, for sure. Especially at first.

But to help heal our kith and kin we must remain steady, and be present.

NEVER FIX

Attempting to fix the hurt in someone versus holding them in their grief is in itself harmful. When we do this we are not seeing them as a whole person with multi-layered experiences, and are instead asking them to move past something incredibly tender so that we don't have to look at it, or experience it with them.

We too often do the same thing with ourselves.

It is near impossible to hear someone's grief without also feeling your own. But when we move through some-thing too soon, we sidestep a key aspect of seeing someone—an acceptance that they, and we, are a whole person whose experiences, tragedies, sorrows, joys, and all, are valid no matter how uncomfortable they make us.

So how do we hold something so nuanced if no one told us how? We start by learning to hold space for this intro-spective and tender witnessing within ourselves.

Go deep
Listen softly
Hold space in silence

LIGHT

It isn't all bad news and tough times.

Though this shared experience is trying, and stretches our own tethers more often than we'd prefer, there is light at the end of tunnel as well.

Often reported by those who are in this deep grief and pain for an extended period, is the transformative, even transcendent experience of spiritual connectedness. In this state, people say they feel a resonant love. They say they feel held up by all the kind words, shared smiles, and kind gestures from all those around them, including people they've never met.

Accompanying someone through this process is a sacred experience. It creates its own form of ceremony and belonging. When done well, these ceremonies of sorrow glow.

They bind.

DISCUSSION TOPICS

1. Have you or someone you know experienced loss recently?
2. How did you process your grief, or help one of your people process their grief?
3. In what ways can you be there for the required healing for a deeper connection?

ACTION TOPICS

1. Listen to a family member without a thought of what you may say in response. What stories are they sharing?
2. Take some time to be in silence today. After a few minutes of quietude, wander around your neighborhood and look for areas that could help a loved one in the grief process? Offer your person a quiet walk in the discovered place.

Chapter 5

------

curating connection - a peace practice

One of the important things to understand in building trust and connection, is that there is a very real cadence to peace. There is a rhythm to the way people speak, how we listen, whether it's the drawn silence or the almost slow-motion absence of expectation. The practice of peace isn't some airy-fairy hope or ungrounded ethereal hogwash. It's tangible. It has quantifiable processes. And you can actually feel the flow of it when you're doing it. As a person who played a lot of sports growing up, I can feel the social flow of peacebuilding in much of the same ways I could feel the game coming to me when I was locked in.

We are beginning to understand more of the neurology behind the processes of this embodied connection, and

with it see the shifts in cognitive and emotional resonance in the brain and hearts of folks when they're
involved in the ways of peace.

In my experiences in participating in cultures of peace I
can say that I have seen these resonances firsthand.
There is a palpable shift in the room. There is sacredness
to the exchange as it murmurs throughout the space.
And a soft whisper begins to be mirrored by those
present. Again, the key here is to learn how to nurture
this process.

To make peace requires a few different skill sets that
effectively facilitate connection. And more often than not
these skills aren't the things you'd think they were. As
stated in the the first chapter, there is no magic way to
solve all problems and conflicts around the world.
However, the skills and practices we'll talk about in this
chapter can set the table for us in nurturing the types of
ways that can most effectively get us on the path of
peace.

SOFT FRAMING

Ironically, the first step required for peacebuilding is not one requiring pursuit, but rather requires the step of letting go of pursuit. Please let me explain. Before we speak, how do we choose to see and understand our relationship with the person or persons we hope to engage with? Where are we, what are we doing, and who are we with? Are they combative? Are they angry? Are they ignorant? And are they insufferable? And how are we? Are we combative, angry, ignorant, and are we insufferable? Conflict and misunderstanding requires multiple people, what is our role in this one?

I know this idea can be a loaded one. Take time to feel your way into it. Have an image of the person you hope to reconcile with in your mind. Now ask the questions above again. Are you framing things correctly, are you exaggerating, or maybe dismissing their perspectives?

The foundation of all of our conflicts, our polarization, our misunderstanding, our othering, and our infighting lay in the nature of how we believe we relate to one another. Before we ever think about whether this or that person/group is with us or against us we need to first see and understand the nature in these relationships. Perhaps the best way to communicate this is to refer to a discussion by Rupert Ross and Leroy Little Bear in Ross's book *Indigenous Healing*. Ross says,

> *. . . Indigenous languages [speak] of the world in ways that emphasize the spiritualized, ethical embeddedness of everything. When I began to look at how these languages described the world, I ran across something written by Leroy Little bear, that I initially found puzzling:*
>
> *Aboriginal paradigms include ideas of constant flux, all existence consisting of energy waves [and] spirit, all things being animate, all existence being interrelated, creation [and] existence having to be renewed, space [and] place as an important referents, and language, songs, stories, and ceremonies as reposi-tories for the knowledge that arise out of these paradigms.*

While I understood much of what he said, I was intrigued by his indication that space and place were important referents in traditional times. In follow-up conversations, Leroy argued that while European languages spoke of the world with time as their central organizing theme, Indigenous languages did not. Instead, they relied on place or space as their central organizing force. (p.41)

Let that sink in a moment . . .

When Indigenous peoples communicate with one another, the central tether to all context revolves around *where* those relationships occurred. Not *when*.

When we look at relationships in this light, we can begin to see how the balance or imbalance in these sets of relationships can influence social process and social outcomes.

Indigenous peoples aren't alone in this particular set of cultural frames, though they may be the most widely used currently. Buddhist thought points us to inter-being. While Quaker teachings focus on interconnectivity. Ubuntu, discussed a few chapters back, also directs us to a shared co-creation. All of this should sound vaguely familiar to you. Think about the idea of interconnection discussed in chapter two.

There are deep practices of interconnectivity woven within and around infrastructures and cultures of peace.

This is no accident.

So before you or I decide to build peace, let us first consider where our feet are, and just who is in front of us.

DEEP LISTENING

It is so easy, too easy, to misunderstand someone.

A couple years ago I was in a depolarization committee group in Nevada County, California. The whole idea of the group was to learn how to listen and speak with folks from different perspectives and life experiences, in this case, with folks that they were not politically aligned with. It was an extension of a Better Angels project. Here they would gather equal members from both blue (democrat) and red (republican) alignments and learn the LAPP process:

Listen-to what the other person says.

Acknowledge-what they said by re-stating it in your own words. Then ask if that is accurate.

Ask **P**ermission to share your own perspective on the topic. And,

Share your **P**erspective.

The LAPP process itself is a good example of active listening. It requires that you're paying attention to what someone has said, while actively tracking the facts and perspectives given. Then finally seeking clarity to make sure you understood them.

Active listening is not enough, however.

While it's true we need to learn how to actively listen, only going this far can still prime a discussion for debate, rather than connection. As study after study has demonstrated, we don't change our minds about things through debate, but rather our minds are changed after our hearts connect in relationship. Debates are often counter-productive and set our mental frames at a default for conflict and in-group protectionism, not toward grounded discussions and problem solving. To really solve the problems in front of us, we need to learn how to deeply listen.

Thich Nhat Hanh, in his highly readable book *The Art of Communicating*, lays out the basics of what deep listening is, how to do it, and why.

He tells us that in the Buddhist tradition, to listen deeply means to help the other person suffer less. Hanh says,

> *When we listen to someone with the intention of helping that person suffer less, this is deep listing. When we listen with compassion, we don't get caught in judgment . . . The other person may say things that are full of wrong perceptions, bitterness, accusation, and blaming. If we don't practice mindfulness, their words will set off irritations, judgment, and anger in us, and we will lose our capacity to listen compassionately. When irritation or anger arises, we lose our*

We've all been in situations where we lost our calm with someone. We became upset, or angry. This is human. It is hard-wired into our primal instincts in the fight or flight response. The sad part is this can be made worse when we haven't yet dealt with our own suffering. Life, being what it is, has dealt us what it has. If we actually want to help the person in front us suffer less, this can be made considerably more difficult if we haven't learned how not to project our own suffering on others. This can understandably become a negative feedback loop. Where despite trying our hardest to listen and be there for our people, our own hang-ups prevent us from being present and vulnerable enough for connection and reconciliation to happen.

Tariq Trotter, from the Roots, calls this the upcycle. In his book, *The Upcylced Self,* he tells his story of the upcycle. We all, because of when and where and how we developed, need to unlearn some of the things we grew up with so we can be with our people in the ways they need. There has been generations of structural violence across all sectors, classes, races, and cultures in society. No one is immune because we are all the same: bounded in shared patterns of connectivity and sorrow, in a shared place.

To listen deeply requires a level of vulnerability so many folks can be afraid of. This is completely understandable. It can be daunting to lay exposed in front of the very people we think have caused us deep harm. The problem is, the conflict cannot be reconciled until we do. The necessary vulnerability of reconciliation requires letting go of control. And a letting go of control, when caught in intergenerational trauma, can seem like giving up.

At the core of this misunderstanding lies a string of lost and knotted truths: listening requires being present, being present requires honest vulnerability, honest vulnerability requires truth, truth requires healing, and healing requires space and shared creation.

A treasured truth across cultures, religions, and philosophies is the simple fact that love comes from understanding. To return back to Mr. Hanh. He prompts us to ask the question, "Do I understand him/her/them enough?" Are we willing to give the time and space necessary to listen deeply, to not just help folks suffer less, but to love well enough to reconcile ourselves?

COMPASSIONATE COMMUNICATION

In that same depolarization committee group years ago, there was once a discussion about where people stood on student loan forgiveness. Were people for it or against it? And why? Two friends, who were on opposite ends of the political spectrum volunteered to be the guinea pigs.

It started off well enough. Each stated their position. Each re-stated the position of the other person, asking if what they said was accurate. Then, almost out of the blue, one of the friends started asking questions in a way that there was no correct answer. "So you believe people shouldn't be held accountable for their own decisions?" "What about the rights and liberties taken away from the taxpayer on what their money goes to?" "What do you think about the ridiculous example this sets for borrowers in the future?" And the like. The core of these questions aren't necessarily bad at all. They center around personal responsibility, freedom, and generally speaking, the good life. The way they are asked leaves much to be desired, though. There was no way their friend could possibly answer their questions without first either conceding an obvious damning point framing them as a guilty and ignorant deplorable, or falling into the positioning and othering based on party platforms, not their own lived experience and perspectives.

Needless to say, it didn't go well.

This is a good example of both listening poorly, and communicating violently. We are all raised and taught to communicate like this in one way or another. It's our collective social default setting.

Returning again to Mr. Hanh. In the Buddhist tradition there is what they call right speech and wrong speech. Right speech or loving speech seeks understanding and to lessen the suffering of the other person. Wrong speech, seeks to misrepresent, other, lie, shifts positions, and stir up conflict. As Mr. Hanh says,

With more understanding, you can really help the other person suffer less, and your communication is more effective. You speak gently because you are willing to help. The way we communicate already makes the other person feel much better.

Right Speech, or compassionate communication, has four core elements:

1 Tell the truth
2 Don't exaggerate
3 Be consistent
4 Use peaceful language

Using these elements of speech to guide how we frame and conduct our conversations goes a long way to laying the groundwork for connection and understanding to occur. We shouldn't use any language that is violent, condemning, abusive, accusing, or judgmental.

A SUMMARY OF THE PEACE PROCESS

We've come a long way in expanding our understanding of not just what peace is, but how to nurture it more in our lives. So let's review the peace process now.

1

Where are your feet?

Literally, where are you standing or sitting? Are you in Rogers Park, Illinois? Or in the unceded traditional homelands of the Three Fires: the Ojibwe, Odawa, and Potawatomi Nations?

Are you in a house, apartment, at work, or in a café or library? As we now know, place matters.

2

Sensory

Is it loud or quiet where you are? Or is it somewhere in-between? Is there natural light? What does the air feel like? Heavy and wet, or dry and cool. Is it hot? When did you last eat? Are you anxious or unsettled? And probably most important, is there visible nature nearby?

As we know, all these things impact how we are going to connect and listen, so what does our body and mind feel like? Are we activated? Or are we present and grounded? Are we even quiet enough internally to hold space for someone else?

3

Deep Listening

Who are you with? How are they feeling? Are they anxious and activated, or are they also grounded centered, and ready to be present? Are they comfortable and relaxed? What kinds of things are they sharing? What isn't being said? What emotions are rising in them? What emotions are rising in you? Did they say something that has activated you? Breath . . . Did you understand what they said correctly? Are you letting silence carry the balance in the conversation? Let the conversation have some air.

4

Compassionate Communication

Restate.

Do you understand what they meant by what they said? How are you speaking with them? When did they last eat? Are they thirsty? First things first. Are you providing a space where they can settle, feel heard, and also feel your openness to them. Are you using right speech and speaking in ways that promote compassion and understanding, or are you using elements of wrong speech and closing down discussion, or waiting to respond with what you want to say rather than hearing what they are saying?

A FEW CONSIDERATIONS

The cadence of peace is a special one. There is a palpable ebb and flow to it. Peace often feels like being held in a warm blanket, while also feeling deeply seen and loved by those around us.

I need to offer a soft warning, though.

There will be much more listening than speaking than the peace process initially lets on. Most folks aren't quite ready to hear our perspectives and opinions on hard topics, even when they say they are. And that's okay. The role of the peacebuilder is to help people feel seen and heard and understood. Hold that space—we can share our thoughts later.

A truly sad part of the negative peace we find ourselves in is that most people never really feel seen. We are all caught in the fray of the day-to-day in one way or another, and rarely take time for ourselves, let alone other people in the ways they need. First we must help people feel seen.

Listen first
Listen second
Then listen again

DISCUSSION TOPICS

1. What do you see as the differences between active listening and deep listening?
2. In what ways do you feel seen and heard?
3. How might you help those around you feel seen?

—

ACTION ITEMS

1. Organize a small listening group to explore ways you might be able to shift community relationships toward liminal peace.
2. The next time you're in a public space, go through the sensory cues in this place. Is it loud or quiet? Is there natural light? Are there plants or green space in view? Are people smiling or avoiding eye contact? Why do you suppose folks are acting the way they are?

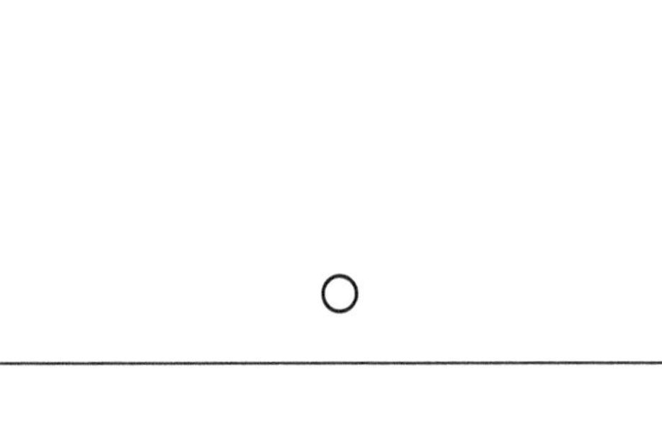

final thoughts

Well done.

I'm proud of you.

We have talked about so many new ideas in such a short amount of time. And you were in it with me for all of it. Thank you for sharing time, space, and hopefully place with me.

Now comes probably the most difficult part of peacebuilding: actually doing the work.

This being said, I know you can do it.

This kind of work is not the work that we can force. Or that any amount of striving could actually help. Making peace, as we have seen over the last few discussions, is more akin to tending a garden. Each plant needs their own nourishment, time, air, and space to grow. And much of the needed growth happens a good deal before we actually see any sprouts.

Yet, we are here for it.

You are more than enough. Be patient with yourself, hold folks in your heart, and move with gentleness and light.

May peace be with you.

CULTURES OF PEACE

Booth, M. (2014). The almost nearly perfect people. Jonathan Cape.

Boulding, E. (1988). Building a global civic culture. Syracuse University Press.

Boulding, E. (2000). Cutlures of peace; the hidden side of history. Syracuse University Press.

Brach, T. (2022). Radical compassion (Part 3): The awakening & realization of belonging. Insight Timer.

Broome, B. (2011). Building relational empathy through an interactive design. In D. Sandole, S. Byrne, I. Staroste-Sandole & J. Senehi (Eds.), Handbook of conflict analysis and resolution (pp. 184-200). Routledge.

Broome, B. (2012). Building cultures of peace: The role of intergroup dialogue. In The Sage handbook of conflict communication: Integrating theory, research, and practice. (pp 737-762). SAGE Publications.

Casmir, F. (1993). Third-culture building: A paradigm shift for international and intercultural communication. Annals of the International Communication Association, 16, 407-428.

CCARE. (2017). Emotional resonance. The Center for Compassion and Altruism Research and Education.

Cherry, K. (2021, March 5). What is the sense of belonging? Very Well Mind.

City of Winnipeg. (2023). Anti-Racism week continues to grow. City of Winnipeg.

Collins, E. (2020, November 30). Francophones of Manitoba. The Canadian Encyclopedia.

Conner, L., Hull, B., Wyatt-Anderson, C., & Seixas, P. (Eds.). (2011). Shaping Canada; our history: from our beginnings to our present. McGraw-Hill Ryerson.

Craft, A. (2021). Treaty words; For as long as the rivers flow. Annick Press.

Dekker, L., & LaRene, P. (December 2006). Go and bring them in. Ensign Magazine.

Di Masso, A. D. (2017). Place attachment, sense of belonging and the micro-politics of place satisfaction. In I. G. Fluery-Bahi, E. Pol, & O. Navarro (Eds.), Handbook of environmental psychology and quality of life research (pp. 85-104). Springer.

Doucette, M., Gladstone, J., & Carter, T. (2021). Indigenous conversational approach to history and business education. Academy of Management Learning & Education, 20(3),

Duany, A., Plater-Zyberk, E., & Speck, J (2000). Suburban nation: The rise of sprawl and the decline of the American dream. North Point Press.

Efron, L. (2022, July 26). What drives a culture of belonging? Gallup.

First Nations Development Institute. (2017). Knowledge center. Strengthening Native American communities and economies. First Nations Development Institute.

Friesen, A. (2022). Screening refugees: Mennonite Central Committee and the postwar environment. Mennonite Quarterly Review, XCVI (3).

Gandhi, M. (1965). Gandhi on nonviolence. New Directions Publishing.

Giessman, H. J. (2016). Embedded peace; Infrastructures for peace: Approaches and Lessons Learned. UNDP.

Glover, T., Todd, J., & Moyer, L. (April 12, 2022). Neighbourhood walking and social connectedness. Fontiers in Sports and Active Living, 4.

Goossen, B. (2017). Chosen nation: Mennonites and Germany in the global era. Princeton University Press.

Hanh, T. (2013). The art of communicating. Harper Collins.

Helliwell, J. L. (2017). World happiness report. World Happiness.

IRCOM. (2022). Home. Immigrant and Refugee Community Organizations of Manitoba.

Kagge, E. (2018). Silence: in the age of noise. Penguin.

Kitchen, P., Williams, A., & Chowhan, J. (2012). Sense of community belonging and health in Canada: A regional analysis. Social Indicators Research.

Klassen-Wiebe, N. (2022, November 15). First Mennonite explores queer theology. Canadian Mennonite.

Lambert, N., Stillman, T., Hicks, J., Kamble, S., Baumeister, R., & Fincham, F. (2013). To belong is to matter: Sense of belonging enhances meaning in life. Personality & social psychology bulletin, 39(11), 1418-1427.

Manzo, L. (2003). Beyond house and have: Toward a revisioning of place attachment. Journal of Environmental Psychology, 47-61.

Maritz, A., Jones, C., Foley, D., & Andrews J. (2022, February 21). Indigenous entrepreneurship may well be the driver of social innovation.The Conversation.

Mennonite Church USA. (2023). Article 22. Peace, justice, and nonresistance. Mennonite Church USA.

Narine, J. (2019, August 12). Social capital and sense of belonging among immigrant groups in Canada. University of Manitoba.

Next Door Inc. (2020, December 2). Global study finds knowing as few as 6 neighbors reduces the likelihood of loneliness. Cision PR Newswire.

Otway, L., & Carnelley, K. (2013). Exploring the associations between adult attachment security and self-actualization and self-transcendence. Self and Identity, 12(2), 217-230.

Painter, C. (2013). Sense of belonging: literature review. Citizenship and Immigration Canada.

Partenan, A. (2016). The Nordic theory of everything. Harper Collins.

Passfield, R. (2018, December 16). Developing trust and your sense of belonging. Grow Mindfullness.

Peace Days. (2022). Who we are. Peace Days.

Penner, C. (2019). Masculinity close to home. In D. Neufeld, & S. Thomas (Eds), Peaceful at heart: Anabaptist reflections on healthy masculinity. (pp. 242-244). Institute of Mennonite Studies.

Petkau, E. R. (2013, October 9) Rethinking peace. Canadian Mennonite. https://canadianmennonite.org/articles/rethinking-peace

Pfeifer, E., & Wittmann. M. (2020). Waiting, thinking, and feeling: Variations in the perception of time during silence. Frontiers in Pyschology.

Ricard, M. (2015). Altruism. Little, Brown and Company.

Rice, B. (2009). Restorative processes of peace and helaing within the governing structures of the Rotinonshonni "Longhouse People". In D. Sandhole, S. Byrne, I Staroste-Sandole, & J. Senehi (Eds.), Handbook of conflict analysis and resolution (pp. 409-419). Routledge.

Ross, R. (2014). Indigneous healing. Penguin Random House.

Turunen, E., & Hiilamo, H. (2022). Sense of belonging

among people outside of working life in Finland. International journal of sociology and social policy.

UVIC Libraries. (2020, February 5). All my relations – Community, respect and reconciliation resources. University of Victoria.

Verzat, V. (2013). Infrastructures for peace: A grass-roots way to do state-building? Berghof Foundation.

Weber, T. (2003). Nonviolence is who? Gene Sharp and Gandhi. Peace & Change, 28(2), 250-270.

Wiking, M. (2016). The little book of hygge; the Danish way to live well. Penguin Random House.

Wiking, M. (2017). The little book of lykke, the Danish search forthe world's happiest people. Penguin Random House.

Wilkinson, R., & Pickett, K. (2019). The inner level; How more equal societies reduce stress, restore sanity and improve everyone's well-being. Penguin Press.

Winnipeg Free Press. (2009, May 6). Festival connects storytelling, peace-building. National Storytelling Festival.

HEALING & RECONCILIATION

Arthur, P. (2011). Memory retrieval and truth recovery. In D. Sandole, S. Byrne, I. Staroste-Sandole, & J. Senehi (Eds.), Handboook of conflict analysis and resolution (pp. 369-382). Routledge.

Bowlby, J. (1969). Attachment and loss Vol. 1: Attachment. Attachment and Loss. Basic books.

Benesch, S. (2022, November 21). Incendiary speech that spurs Viovence is rising in US, but tools exist to shrink it.

Black, J. (2023). The ReDress Project. Jaime Black.

Bowman, B., Fuith, J. (April 2022). Winnipeg's path to reconciling systemic inequity: Acknowledge. Listen. Act. How cities can transform to lead the way in combating racism. The Brooking's Institute.

Buergelt, P., Mahypilama, L., Paton, D., (2022, October 19). The Value of Sophisticated Indigenous Ways of Being-Knowing-Doing Towards Transforming Human Resource Development in Ways that Contribute to Organizations Thriving and Addressing Our Existential Crises. Human Resource Development Review, 21(4).

Byrne, S. (2017). The legacy of colonialism among Indigenous peoples: Destructive outcomes, healing and reconciliatory potentials. Peace Research: Canadian Journal of Peace and Conflict Studies, 49(2), 5-13.

Canada. (2022, November 11). Delivering on Truth and Reconciliation Commission calls to action. Government of Canada.

Canada. (2023). Canadian heritage. Government of Canada.

Circles for Reconciliation. (2022). What we do. Circles for Reconciliation.

Coates, T.N. (2017). We were eight years in power; an American tragedy. BCP Literary, Inc.

Eddo-Lodge, R. (2017). Why i'm no longer talking to white people about race. Bloomsbury Publishing Plc.

Fast, M. (2013). Making a way when there is no way : The experiences and challenges of gang affected young adult refugees in Winnipeg. University of Manitoba. Arthur V. Mauro Institute for Peace and Justice.

First Step Alliance. (2022, January 3). What we can learn from Norway's prison system: Rehabilitation & recidivism. First Step Alliance.

Fisher, D.R. (2022, July 22). Lesson learned from the George Floyd protests. The Brookings Institute.

Franko, W., & Witko, C. (2017). Growing inequality and public awareness of inequality in the States. DOI, 50–72

Government of Canada. (2023). About the Truth and Reconciliation Commission.

Government of Canada. (2023). Sayisi Dene First Nation relocation claim.

Hart, D. (2016). Trouble i've seen: Changing the way the church views racism. Herald Press.

Harvest Manitoba, (2022). Harvest voices; Stories of hunger and poverty in Manitoba.

Heritage, C. (2022). Government of Canada supports

projects across Canada to commemorate the National Day for Truth and Reconciliation. Canada.ca.

Kelman, H. C. (2008). Reconciliation from a social-psychological perspective. In A. Nadler, T.E. Malloy, & J.D. Fisher (Eds.), The social psychology of intergroup reconciliation (pp 15-32). Oxford University Press.

Kendi, I.X. (2019). How to be an anti-racist. Random House Publishing.

Koop, K. (2023, May 8). What are we reckoning with and how? The context of our questions. CMU Faculty Retreat. Canadian Mennonite University.

Lutschini, M. (2005). Engaging with holism in Australian Aboriginal health policy – a review. Australian New Zealand Health Policy.

Manitoba Harvest. (2022). We are a harvest community; Harvest Manitoba gratitude report 2021-2022.

Manitoba Healing Centre. (1994). Manitoba joint committee on residential schools 1994 proposal. edited by Joint working committee. Manitoba: Manitoba healing resource centre for first nations affected by residential schools.

Maritz, A., Jones, C., Foley, D., & Andrews J. (2022, February 21). Indigenous entrepreneurship may well be the driver of social innovation.The Conversation.

Mehta, D., Bruenig, D., Pierce, J., Sathyanarayanan, A., Stringfellow, R., Miller, O., Mullens, A., & Shakespeare-Finch, J. (2022). Recalibrating the epigenetic clock after exposure to trauma: The role of risk and protective psychosocial factors. Journal of Psychiatric Research, 374-381.

MOTR. (2023). Chapter 1. Mothers of the Resistance; Red River Métis Geneologies:

MyPEG. (2022, February 8). 2021 Voluntary local review shares Winnipeg progress with United Nations. MyPEG.

MyPEG. (2022). Winnipeg and the SDGs: A voluntary local review of progress 2021.

National Centre for Truth and Reconciliation. (2023). History of the TRC. National Centre for Truth and Reconciliation.

National Centre for Truth and Reconciliation. (2023). Residential schools. National Centre for Truth and Reconciliation. https://nctr.ca/education/teaching-resources/residential-school-history/

Penner, C. (2017). Sacred trust . . fostering safe spaces in congregations; A resource for the Anabaptist faith community on sexual misconduct in the church. Mennonite Church Eastern Canada.

Ramaujam, A., Asri, N., & Wahlgren, J. (2021). The climate crisis is a neocolonial capitalist crisis: Expereinces, responses and steps towards decolonising climate action. ENAR.

Red River Polytech. (2023). Indigenous student supports and community relations. Red River Polytech.

Romero, J. (2023). Women are sacred. Coalition to Stop Violence Against Native Women.

Taylor, D.B. (2021, November 5). George Floyd Protests: A Timeline. The New York Times.

Tennant, P. (2021). "We live in different worlds": The perspectives of Manitoba educators on settler colonialism, Indigenous-settler relations, and reconciliation. University of Manitoba.

The Equality Trust. (2010). Embracing the Spirit Level from the political right.

The National Indigenous Women's Resource Centre. (2022). 2022 National Week of Action for MMIW.

The Truth Commission into Genocide in Canada. (2001). Hidden from History: The Canadian Holocaust. British Columbia.

TRCB. (2017, May 4). All my relations. Truth and Reconciliation Community Bobcaygeon.

United Nations. (2023). United Nations Declaration on the Rights of Indigenous Peoples . United Nations.

United Nations Division for the Advancement of Women (2005, October). Equal participation of women and men in decision-making processes, with particular emphasis on political participation and leadership. United Nations.

MEASURING PEACE

Allen, K. A. (2021). The psychometric evaluation of the sense of belonging instrument with Iranian older adults. BMC Geriatrics.

American Heart Association. (2022, July 25). New study finds lowest risk of death was among adults who exercised 150-600 minutes/week. Science Daily.

American Heart Association. (2017). Heart disease and stroke statistics-2017. American Heart Association.

Andolina, M., Keeter, S., Zukin, C., Jenkins, K. (Eds.). (2003). A guide to the index of civic and political engagement. The Center for Information & Research on Civic Learning & Engagement.

Bush, K. (2009). Aid for peace: A handbook for applying peace and conflict impact assessment (PCIA). Univeristy of Ulster and United Nations University.

City of Winnipeg. (2023). Winnipeg parks and open space. Parkmaps.

Deiner, E. S. (1997). Measuring quality of life: Economic, social, and subjective indicators. Social Indicators Research, 189-216.

Culdesac. (2021, May 7). Walkability and happiness. Culdesac.

Diener, E. (2017). Measuring quality of life: Economic, social, and subjective indicators. Social Indicators Research 40, 189-216.

Foodbanks Canada. (2016). Hunger count 2016. A comprehensive report on hunger and food bank use in

Canada, and recommendations for change. Foodbanks Canada.

Galtung, J. (2016, July 11). Charlatanism: The positive peace index. Transcend.

Garone, S. (2021, September 23). 8 Physical and mental health benefits of silence. Healthline.

Glover, T., Todd, J., & Moyer, L. (April 12, 2022). Neighbourhood walking and social connectedness. Fontiers in Sports and Active Living, 4.

Hagerty, B., & Patusky, K. (1995). Developing a measure of sense of belonging. Nursing Research, 44(1), 9-13.

Lindsay, P., Figuierodo, A. C., & Byrne, S. (2022). The abcs of measuring positive peace. In K. D. Standish, H. Devere, A. Suazo, & R. Rafferty (Eds.), The Palgrave handbook of positive peace (pp. 369-414). Palgrave MacMillan.

Mac Ginty, R. (2012). Indicators +: A proposal for everday peace indicators. Evaluation and Program Planning, 57-60.

Mac Ginty, R. (2020). (Eds.), Alternative and bottom-up peace indicators. Routledge.

ODI. (2018). Political voice and elections. ODI.

O'Donnell, V., & Wallace, S. (2011, July). First Nations, Inuit, and Metis women. Statistics Canada. Women in Canada; A gender-based statistical report.

OECD. (2016, July 22). Universal health coverage and health outcomes.

OECD. (2018). Better life index. Civic Engagement.

OECD. (2018). Employment rate. OECD.

OECD. . (2018). Safety. Better Life Index.

Sandole, D. (2013). Extending the reach of basic human needs. In K. Avruch (Ed.), Conflict resolution and human needs. Routledge.

Scrivens, K., & Iasiello, B. (2010, June 30). Indicators of societal progress: Lessons learned from international experiences. OECD.

Turcotte, M. (2015, September 14). Civic engagement and political participation in Canada. Statistics Canada.

PEACE & CONFLICT STUDIES

Ahmed, K. (2017). Social conflict and peace-building: The perceptions, experiences, and contributions of leaders of selected community-based organizations in Winnipeg, Manitoba. University of Manitoba

Allen, S. (2022). Interactive peacemaking; A people-centred approach. Routledge.

Arias, M. L. (2018). How humans predict behaviour; And why this matters to practitioners! BehaviouralEconomics.com.

Barkwell, L. (2014). Contributions Made by Métis People. Louis Riel Institute.

Birch, K. (2017, November 2). What exactly is neoliberalism? The Conversation.

Bogdan, R.C., & Biklen, S.K. (Eds.). (2007). Qualitative research for education: An introduction to theory and methods. Pearson Education, Inc.

Bonisch, A. (1981). Elements of the modern concept of peace. Journal of Peace Research, 18, (2)

Bresinger, G. (2016). The great inflation of the 1970s.

Britannica. (2023). Supply and demand. Britannica.

Brown, M. (2013). Anthropology and peacebuilding. In R. Mac Ginty (Eds.), Routledge handbook of peacebuilding (pp. 132-146). Routledge.

Burton, J. (1990). Conflict: A human needs theory. St. Martin's Press.

Byrne, S., & Carter, N. (1996). Social cubism: Six social

forces of ethnoterritorial conflict in northern Ireland and Quebec. Peace and Conflict Studies, 3(2): 52-71.

Byrne, S., Carter, N., & Senehi, J. (May 2003). Social cubism and social conflict: Analysis and Resolution. Journal of International and Comparative Law, 8(3):725-740.

Byrne, S., & Nadan, A. (May 2011). Inside the social cube: Framing and understanding the Israeli-Palestinian and Northern Ireland conflicts. In Matyok, T., Senehi, J., Byrne, S.

(Eds.) Critical Issues in Peace and Conflict Studies: Implications for Theory, Practice, and Pedagogy. (pp. 61-80). Lexington Books.

Byrne, S., & Thiessen, C. (2020). Foreign peacbuilding intervention and emancipatory local agency for social justice. In S. Byrne, T. Matyok, I.M. Scott & J. Senehi (Eds.), Routledge companion to peace and conflict studies. (pp. 131-142). Routledge.

Carter, N., & Byrne, S. (2000). The dynamics of social cubism: A view from Northern Ireland and Quebec. In Byrne, S., & Irvin, C.; Dixon,P., Polkinghorn, B., Senehi, J. (Eds.) Reconcilable differences: Turning points in ethnopolitical conflicts. (pp.41-65). Kumarian Press.

CDC. (2023). Public health action guide. CDC.

Clarke, A., Friese, C., & Washburn, R. (2018). Situational analysis in practice: Mapping research with grounded theory. Left Coast Press.

Cline, E. (2016, February 16). The power of buying less by buying better. The Atlantic.

CMHR. (2023). About. Canadian Museum for Human Rights.

Cook-Hoffman, C. (2011). The role of identity on conflict. In D.Sandole, S. Byrne, I. Staroste-Sandole, & J. Senehi (Eds.), Handbook of conflict analysis and resolution (pp. 20-31). Routledge.

Cook-Hoffman, C. (2015, March 24). Identity matters: Confronting identity on the road to conflict resolution, peace and justice. MLT Aikins St. Paul's College University Affiliation Lecture. University of Manitoba.

Friends of CMHR. (2019, December 3). The power and importance of the Canadian Museum of Human Rights. Friends of CMHR.

Friere, P. (1972). Pedagogy of the oppressed. Herder and Herder.

Galtung, J. (1996). Peace by peaceful means: Peace and conflict, development and civilization. Sage.

Giddens, A. (1991). Modernity and self-identity: Self and society in the late modern age. Stanford University Press.

Grewal, B. S. (2003, August 30). Johann Galtung, negative and positive peace. Active for Peace.

Hart Research Associates. (2020). Politics of identity and othering 2020. Center for Voter Information.

Henshilwood, C. M. (2003). The origin of modern human behavior: Critique of the models and their test implications. Current Anthropology. 44, 627–651.

Keyes, C. (2007). Promoting and protecting mental health as flourishing. American Psychologist, 95-108.

King, Jr., Martin Luther. (1992, [1963]). Letter from a Birmingham jail. In J. Fahey & R. Armstrong (Eds.). A peace reader (pp. 113–128). Paulist.

Lederach, J. (1995). Preparing for peace. Syracuse University Press.

Mac Ginty, R. (2007). No war, no peace: The rejuvenation of stalled peace processes and peace accords. Palgrave Macmillan.

Mac Ginty, R. (2010). Hybrid peace: The interaction between top-down and bottum-up peace. Security and Dialogue, 391-412.

Mac Ginty, R. (Ed.). (2013). Routledge handbook of peacebuilding. Routledge.

Mac Ginty, R. (2022). Everyday peace: How so-called ordinary people can disrupt violence. Oxford University Press.

Madden, B. (2010). Being ethnographic: A guide to the theory and practice of ethnography. SAGE Publications, Inc.

Maslow, A. (1943). A theory of human motivation. Psychological Review. 50 (4), 370–396.

Matza, D. (1969). On Becoming Deviant. Prentice Hall.

McBrearty, S. B. (2000). The revolution that wasn't: A new interpretation of the origin of modern human behavior. Journal of Human Evolution. 39, 453–563.

Nan, S. A. (2003). Intervention coordination. Beyond Intractibility. https://www.beyondintractability.org/essay/intervention_coordination.

Newman, E. (2013). The international architecture of peacebuilding. In R. Mac Ginty, Routledge handbook of peacebuilding (pp. 311-324). Routledge.

Paris, R. (2010). Saving liberal peacebuilding. Review of International Studies, 36(2), 337-365.

Peace Magazine. (2015, December 24). Gene Sharp, 101, 2003

Pichler, M. (2011). Culture formation and endogenous cultural distance. Center for Mathematical Economics.

Pugh, M. (2005). The political economy of peacebuilding: A critical theory perspective. International Journal of Peace Studies, 10(2).

Pugh, M. (2013). The problem solving and critical paradigms. In R. Mac Ginty (Eds.), Routledge handbook of peacebuilding (pp. 11-24). Routledge.

Putnam, R. (2000). Bowling alone. Simon & Schuster.

Reimer, L., Schmitz, L., Janke, E., Askerov, A., Strahl, B., & Matyok, T. (Eds.). (2015). Transformative change: An introduction to peace and conflict studies. Lexington Books.

Rothman, J. (1997). Resolving identity-based conflict: In nations, organizations, and communities. Jossey-Bass Publishers.

Russell, J. (1980). A circumplex model of affect. Journal of Personality and Social Psychology, 1161-1178.

Schmid, H. (1968). Peace research and politics. Journal of Peace Research, Volume 5, Issue 3.

Senehi, J. (2011). Building peace; Storytelling to transform conflicts constructively. In D. Sandole, S. Byrne, I.

Staroste-Sandole, & J. Senehi (Eds.), Handbook of conflict analysis and resolution (pp. 201-214). Routledge.

Senehi, J. (2020). Theory-building in peace and conflict studies: The storytelling methodology. In S. Byrne, T. Matyok, I.M. Scott & J. Senehi (Eds.), Routledge companion to peace and conflict studies. (pp. 45-57). Routledge.

Sharp, G. (1993). From dictatorship to democracy. Green Print Housmans.

Skey, M. (2011). National belonging and everyday life: The significance of nationhood in an uncertain world. Palgrave Macmillan.

Soto Parra, E. (2018). Peacebuilding: Quixote House and the reintegration into community of released offenders. University of Manitoba.

Standish, K., Devere, H., Suazo, A., & Rafferry, R. (Eds.). (2022). The Palgrave handbook of positive peace. Palgrave MacMillan.

Steinberg, G. (2013). The limits of peacebuilding theory. In R. Mac Ginty, Routledge handbook of peacebuilding (pp. 36-53). Routledge.

Strochein, S. (2013). Organic versus strategic approached to peacebuilding. In R. Mac Ginty, Routledge handbook of peacebuilding (pp. 276-286)). Routledge.

Sunstein, C. (2016). The ethics of influence. Cambridge University Press.

Thiessen, C. & Byrne, S. (2017). Proceed with caution: Research production and uptake in conflict-affected countries. Journal of Peacebuilding & Development, 13(1), 1-15.

UNDP. (2015). Sustainable development goals. United Nations Development Program.

United Nations. (2016). The Universal Declaration of Human Rights. United Nations.

United Nations. (2017). Human Rights Office of the Commissioner. Statement on visit to the USA, by Professor Philip Alston, United Nations special rapporteur on extreme poverty and human rights. United Nations.

Ury, W. (2000). The third side: Why we fight and how we can stop. Peguin Random House.

Wanis-St. John, A. (2013). Indigenous peacebuilding. In R. Mac Ginty, Routledge handbook of peacebuilding (pp. 360-374). Routledge.

Woodward, E. (2013). The political economy of peacebuilding and international aid. In R. Mac Ginty, Routledge handbook of peacebuilding (pp. 325-335). Routledge.

Zimbardo, P. (2016). Stanford prison experiment. Stanford University.

SOCIAL INNOVATION

Bornstein, D., & Davis, S. (2010). Social entrepreneurship; What everyone needs to know. Oxford University Press.

Couture, J. (2013). A metaphorical mind. Athabasca University Press.

Creswell, W. (2012). Educational research: Planning, conducting and evaluating quantitative and qualitative research. Pearson.

Friere, P. (1972). Pedagogy of the oppressed. Herder and Herder.

Hasso Plattner Institute of Design. (2023). The d school. Stanford University.

Homan, M. (2011). Promoting community change; Making it happen in the real world. Brooks/Cole.

Kavanagh, S. (2021, April 23). First in: Winnipeg social enterprise activist Shaun Loney announces 2022 mayoral run. CBC.

Lawler, E. (2014, May 7). The quadruple bottom line: Its time has come. Forbes.

Leech, N., & Onwuegbuzie, A. (2007). An array of qualitative data analysis tools: A call for data analysis triangulation. Social Psychology Quarterly, 22(4), 557-584.

Lindgaard, K. W. (2017, May 1). Once more, with feeling: Design thinking and embodied cognition. CDN.com.

Loney, S. (2016). An army of problem solvers: Reconciliation and the solutions economy. Friesens.

Loney, S. (2018). The beautiful bailout. The Harbinger Foundation.

Malena, C. H. (2007). Can we measure civil society? A proposed methodology for international comparative research. Development in Practice, 17(3), 338-352.

Maritz, A., Jones, C., Foley, D., & Andrews J. (2022, February 21). Indigenous entrepreneurship may well be the driver of social innovation.The Conversation.

McSweeny, K. (2020, March 26). Complex systems theory: How science solves social issues. Northrup Grumman.

Mihas, P. (2019). Qualitative data analysis. Oxford University Press.

Miller, K. (2020, December 8). The triple bottom line: What it is and why it's important. Harvard Budiness School Online.

Neuberg, S. K. (2018). Evolutionary social psychology. UBC Psychology.

Ormston, R., Spencer, L., Barnard, M., & Snape, D. (2014). The foundations of qualitative research. Qualtiative research practice: a guide for social science students and researchers, 2, 52-55.

Piketty, T. (2014). Capital in the twenty-first century. The Belknap Press of Harvard University Press.

Reid, C., Greaves, L., & Kirby, S. (Eds.). (2017). Experience, research, social change, 3rd Edition. University of Toronto.

Rodriguez, L. (2019, January 5). 5 reasons for measuring social impact in social enterprise. SOPACT.

Saldana, J. (2021). The coding manual for qualitative researchers. Sage.

Silver, J. (2016). Solving poverty; Innovative strategies from Winnipeg's inner city. Fernwood Publishing.

Social Change Central. (2023). How to measure and report your social impact. Social Change Central.

Thaler, R. S., & Sunstein, C. (2009). Nudge; Improving decisions about health, wealth, and happiness. Penguin.

Thomas, D. (2006). A general inductive approach for analyzing qualitative evaluative data. American Journal of Evaluation, 27(2), 237-246.

Thurner, S., Klimec, P., & Hanel, R. (2018). Introduction to the theory of complex systems. Oxford University Press.

Wates, N. (2008). The community planning event manual; How to use collaborative planning and urban design events to improve your environment. Earthscan Publications LTD.

Woo, S. E. (2017). Best Practices in Developing, Conducting, and Evaluating Inductive Research. Human Resource Management Review, 27, 255-264.

ACRP. (2017). Effects of aircraft noise on student performance; understanding noise, its effects on learning, and what can be done about it.

Adams, R. (2009). From industrial cities to eco-urbanity: the Melbourne case study. In D. Radovic, Eco-urbanity; Towards well-mannered built environments. Routledge.

Aghostin-Sangar, V. (2007, February 23). Human behaviour in public spaces. University of South Wales.

Alexander, C. (1979). The timeless way of building. Oxford University Press.

Anjali, J. (2006). Impact of light on outcomes in healthcare settings. The Center for Health Design.

ARUP. (2016, June). Cities alive; Toward a walking world.

ASCE. (2018). 2017 Infrastructure report card. American Society of Civil Engineers.

Australian Academy of Science. (2023). Health effects of environmental noise pollution. Science.org.au.

Ayers, E. (2010). Turning toward place, space, and time. In D. C. Bodemhamer, The spatial humanities: GIS and the future of humanities scholarship (pp. 1-13). Indiana University Press.

B'Ber Architects. (2018). The importance of public space. B'Ber Architects.

Be Offices. (2018, February 5). Daylight in the workplace – Are we getting enough?

Bickard, M. (2018). How does the environment affect the person? . In L. V. Winegar, Children's development within social contexts: Metatheoretical, theoretical and methodological issues.

Bjorkdahl, A. (2016). Spatializing peace and conflict; Mapping the production of places, sites and scales of violence. Palgrave MacMillan.

Bodenhamer, D. (2015). Deep maps and spatial narratives. Indiana University Press.

Bollens, S. (2012). City and soul in divided societies. Routledge.

Bollens, S. (2013). Urban planning and policy. In R. M. Ginty, Routledge handbook of peacebuilding (pp. 375-386). Routledge.

Boyson, O. (2016). The future of cities. Youtube.

Budds, D. (2016, September 17). Parks that are making their cities more beautiful— and sustainable; Here's how Thomas Woltz and company channel site-specific details into meaningful, large-scale parks. Fast Company.

Burga, H. (2008). Traditions of placemaking and fundamentalisms of practice: the new urbanism in the context of globalization. Traditional Dwellings and Settlements Review, 20(1), 15-15.

Bush, J. (2020). Nature in place: placemaking in the biosphere. In D. Hes, C. Hernandez-Santin (Eds.), Placemaking fundamentals for the built environment (pp. 39-62). Palgrave Macmillan.

Buxton, R. (2021). A synthesis of health benefits of

natural sounds and their distribution in national parks. Environmental Sciences.

Castello, L. (2016). Rethinking the meaning of place: Conceiving place in architecture-urbanism. Routledge.

Celis-Morales, C., Lyall, D., Welsh, P., Anderson, J., Steell, L., Guo, Y., & Maldonado, R. (2017). Association between active commuting and incident cardiovascular disease, cancer, and mortality: prospective cohort study. BMJ.

Chatterjee, K., Chang, S., Clark, B., Davis, D., De Vos, J., Ettema, D., & Handy, S. (2019, August 1). Commuting and wellbeing: a critical overview of the literature with implications for policy and future research. Transport Reviews, 40, 5-34.

Cities of Peace. (2023). How to establish a city of peace. Cities of Peace.

City of Barcelona. (2014). Urban mobility plan of barcelona PMU 2013-2018. City of Barcelona.

City of Winnipeg. (2022). Our Winnipeg 2045 development plan. City of Winnipeg.

CityLab. (2023). About. Bloomberg Cities Network.

Clos, O. (2009). The Barcelona agenda: Reuse, compactness and green. In D.

Radovic (Ed.), Eco-urbanity; Towards well-mannered built environments. Routledge.

Collado, S. (2017). Restorative environments and health. In G. Fluery-Bahi, E. Pol, & O.

Navarro (Eds.), Handbook of environmental

psychology and quality of life research (pp. 127-148). Springer.

Comerio, M. (1984). Community design: Idealism and entrepreneurship. Journal of Architectural and Planning Research, 1(4), 227-243.

Cooper, S. S. (2015, October). Addressing core housing need in Canada. Canadian Centre for Policy Alternatives.

Creagh, R., Babb, C., & Farley, H. (2020). Local governments and developers in placemaking: defining their responsibilities and capacities to shape place. In D. Hes, C. Hernandez-Santin (Eds.), Placemaking fundamentals for the built environment (pp. 107-128). Palgrave Macmillan.

Culdesac. (2021, May 7). Walkability and happiness. Culdesac.

Denmark. (2023). A nation of cyclists. Denmark.dk.

Deprés, C. P. (2017). Linking people-environment research and design. What's missing? In G. P. Fleury-Bahi (Ed.), Hanbook of environmental pysychology and quality of life research (pp. 65-83). Springer.

Di Masso, A. D. (2017). Place attachment, sense of belonging and the micro-politics of place satisfaction. In I. G. Fluery-Bahi, E. Pol, & O. Navarro (Eds.), Handbook of environmental psychology and quality of life research (pp. 85-104). Springer.

Dieleman, F., & Wegener, M. (2004). Compact city and urban sprawl. Built Environment , 308-323.

Duke, J. (2009). Mixed income housing policy and

public housing residents' 'right to the city'. Critical Social Policy, 29(1),

Dutchen, S. (Spring 2021). The effects of noise on health. Noise pollution is more than a nuisance, it's a health risk. Harvard Medical School. Harvard Medicine.

Elredge, B. (2016, October 17). How a parking tax can build better public transit; Nottingham, England's controver- sial parking tax has brought two new tram lines and more robust public infrastructure to the city. Curbed.

Everett, P. W. (1987). Psychological contributions to transportation. In D. Stokols (Ed.), Handbook of environmental psychology (pp. 987-1008). Wiley.

Fitzgerlad, S. (2019, October 18). The secret to mindful travel? A walk in the woods. National Geographic.

Fluery-Bahl, G., Pol, E., & Navarro, O. (Eds.). (2017). Handbook of environmental psychology and quality of life research. Springer.

Garone, S. (2021, September 23). 8 Physical and mental health benefits of silence. Healthline.

Glover, T., Todd, J., & Moyer, L. (April 12, 2022). Neighbourhood walking and social connectedness. Fontiers in Sports and Active Living, 4.

Godman, H., & Komaroff, A. (2023, June 1). Better together: The many benefits of walking with friends. Harvard Health Letter. Harvard Health Publishing.

Goldhagen, S. (2017). Welcome to your world, How the built environment shapes our lives. Harper Collins.

Grandjean, E. G. (1976). Environmental factors in urban planning: Air pollution, noise, urban open spaces, sunlight and natural lighting indoors. Taylor and Francis.

Graziano, M. (2018). The spaces between us; A story of neuroscience, evolution, and human nature. Oxford University Press.

Greenfield, E., & Reyes, J. (2015, July). Continuity and change in relationships with neighbors: Implications for psychological well-being in middle and later life. The Journals of Gerontology: Series B, 70(4), 607–618.

Happy Cities. (2023). Walkability. Happy Cities.

Hes, D., Hernandez-Santin, C., Beer, T., & Huang, S. (2020). Place evaluation: Measuring what matters by prioritising relationships. In D. H.-S. Hes (Eds), Place-making fundamentals for the built environment (pp. 294-322). Palgrave Macmillan.

Hes, D., Soderlund, J., Desha, C., & Pidcock, C. (2018). Natural connectors: Biophilic design takes root. Sanctuary: Modern Green Homes, 45, 68–73.

Hubbard, P., Kitchin, R., & Valentine, G. (Eds.). (2008). Key texts in human geography. Sage

Ittelson, W. P. (1974). An introduction to environmental psychology. Holt, Reiner and Winston.

James, P., Banay, R., Hart, J., & Laden F. (2015). A review of the health benefits of greenness. Curr Epidemiol Rep. Jun;2(2), 131-142.

Jennings, V., & Bamkole, O. (2019). The relationship between social cohesion and urban green space: an avenue for health promotion. International Journal of Environmental Res Public Health 16(3)

Jiang, Y., Lic, M., & Chung, T. (2023, January). Living alone and all-cause mortality in community-dwelling older adults: The moderating role of perceived neighborhood cohesion. Social Science & Medecine, 317.

Joye, Y. (2011). Biophilic design aesthetics in art and design education. The Journal of Aesthetic Education, 45(2), 17–35.

Küller, R. (1992). Environmental assessment from a neuropsychological perspective. In T. E. Gärling (Ed.), Environment, cognition, and action: an integrated approach (pp. 111-147). Oxford University Press.

Kopec, D. (2006). Environmental psychology for design. Fairchild Publications Inc.

Kulwich, R. (2008, November 12). Going out on a limb with a tree-person ratio. National Public Radio.

Larson, L., & Hipp, J. (2022). Nature-based pathways to health promotion: The value of parks and greenspace. North Carolina Medical Journal,

Lebrument, N., Zumbu-Lebrument, C., Rochette, C., & Roulet, T. (2021). Triggering participation in smart cities: Political efficacy, public administration satisfaction and sense of belonging as drivers of citizens' intention. Technological Forecasting and Social Change. 171.

Leyden, K. (2003). Social capital and the built environment: The importance of walkable neighborhoods. American Journal of Public Helath, 1546–1551.

Lindsay, P. (2024). Spatial peace. Cities. Elsevier. Vol. 155.

Loh, C., Ashley, A., Kim, R., Durham, L., & Bubb, K. (2022). Placemaking in practice: Municipal arts and cultural plans' approaches to placemaking and creative placemaking. Journal of Planning Education and Research , 1-12.

Lyndon, M., & Garcia, A. (2015). Tactical urbanism: Short-term actions for long-term change. Island Press.

Mahmoud, I. (2022). Placemaking for green urban regeneration. Springer.

Manohar, P. (2011, January 15). The high density advantage. Liveable Cities Think Tank.

Manzo, L. (2003). Beyond house and have: Toward a revisioning of place attachment. Journal of Environmental Psychology, 47-61.

Mateo-Babiano, I. (2020). People in place: Placemaking fundamentals . In G. Lee, Placemaking fundamentals for the built environment (pp. 15–38). Springer.

Mazzoni, M. (2016, October 17). Design justice: Creating inclusive spaces in an urbanized world. Triple Pundit. https://www.triplepundit.com/story/2016/design-justice-creating-inclusive-spaces-urbanized-world/22091

Milgrom, R. (2003). Sustaining diversity: Participatory Design and the Production of Urban Space. York University, Faculty of Environmental Studies.

Milgrom, R. (2016, April 11). Community processes. (P. Lindsay, Interviewer)

Montgomery, A. (2016). Reappearance of the public: Placemaking, minoritization and resistance in Detroit. International Journal of Urban and Regional Research, 40(4), 776-799.

Nursey-Bray, M. (2020). The ART of engagement placemaking for nature and people in cities. In D. Hes, & C. Hernandez-Santin (Eds.), Placemaking fundamentals for the built environmet (pp. 305-326). Palgrave Macmillan.

Olivos, P. C. (2017). Self, nature and well-being: Sense and connectedness and environmental identity for quality of life. In G. Fluery-Bahi, E. Pol, & O. Navarro (Eds.), Handbook of environmental psychology and quality of life research (pp. 107-126). Springer.

Pena, C. (2021, May 4). 10 years of research reveals that listening to nature can improve your overall health. My Modern Met.

Perfect, M. P. (2014). Planning for urban quality: Urban design in towns and cities. Routledge.

Planella, A. B. (2019). Barcelona gives way to green infrastructure. Barcelona gives way to green infrastructure.

Pol, E. (2017). Quality of life and sustainability: The end of quality at any price. In G. Fluery-Bahi, E. Pol, O. Navarro (Eds.), Handbook of environmental psychology and quality of life research (pp. 11-40). Springer.

Radovic, D. (2009). Eco-urbanity; towards a well-mannered built environment. Routledge.

Relph, E. (2008). Place and placelessness. In D. Seamon (Ed.), Key texts in human geography (pp. 43-51).

Roberts, L. (2016). Deep mapping. Printed Edition of the Special Issue Published in Humanities.

Sampson, R. (2003). The neighborhood context of well-being. Perspectives in Biology and Medicine, 53-64. Harvard.

Scanell, L., & Gifford, R. (2010). Defining place attachment: A tripartite organizing framework. Journal of Environmental Psychology, 30(1), 1-10.

Scanell, L., & Gifford, R. (2014). The psychology of place attachment. In R. Gifford (Eds.), Environmental psychology: Principles and practice edition: 5th (pp. 272-300). Optimal Books.

Shamai, S. (1991). Sense of place: An empirical measurement. Geoforum 22(3), 347-358.

Shwab, K. (2019, April 11). What is biophilic design, and can it really make you happier and healthier? Fast Company.

Sim, D. (2009). The sustainable city as a fine-grained city.. In D. Radovic (Eds), Eco-urbanity; Towards well-mannered built environments. Routledge.

Sipe, N. (2020). Economics of place. In D. Hes, C. Hernandez-Santin (Eds.). Placemaking fundamentals for the built environment (pp. 157-176). Palgrave Macmillan.

Smith, P. (1977). The syntax of cities. Hutchinson & Co.

Springett, S. (2016). Going deeper of flatter: Connecting deep mapping, flat ontologies and the democratization of knowledge. MDPI Printed Edition of the Special Issue Published in Humanities.

SPUTNIC. (August 2009). Guidelines in market organization: Public transport integration. European Commission. Strategies for Public Transport in Cities. 6th Framework Programme.

Steuteville, R. (2021, August 12). Ten social benefits of walkable places. CNU.

Stokols, D. Lejano, R., & Hipp, J. (2013). Enhancing the resilience of human-environment systems: A social ecological perspective. Ecology and Society.

Tapia-Fonllem, C. C. (2017). Sustainable behavior and quality of life. In G. Fleury-Bahi, E. Pol, O Navarro (Eds.), Handbook of environmental psychology and quality of life research (pp. 173-184). Springer.

The World Bank Group. (2018). CO2 emissions.

The World Bank Group. (2020). Urban development.

Tidball, K. (2012). Urgent biophilia: Human-nature interactions and biological attractions in disaster resilience. Ecology and Society,17(2).

Toolis, E. (2017). Theorizing critical placemaking as a tool for reclaiming public space. American Journal of Community Psychology, 59(1-2), 184-199.

Trejo, F. (2012). Community rejuvenation through placemaking initiatives; Planners, famers' markets and urban neighbourhoods, Central Park neighbourhood, Winnipeg, Canada. University of Manitoba.

UNEP. (2019, June 11). Cycling, the better mode of transport. United Nations Environment Program.

United Nations. (1994). An agenda for development.

United Nations. (2017). Shanghai manual-a guide for sustainable urban development in the 21st century. United Nations.

Valera, S. V. (2017). Some cues for a positive environmental pychology agenda. In G. Fluery-Bahi, E. Pol, O. Navarro (Eds.), Handbook of environmental psycbology and quality of life research (pp. 41-63). Springer.

Veitch, J. A. (2012). Work environments. In S. D. Clayton, The Oxford handbook of environmental and conservation psychology (pp. 248–275). Oxford University Press.

Velux. (2023). 1.9 Daylight requirements in building codes. Velux .

WHO. (2016). Urban green spaces and health; a review of the evidence. World Health Organization.

Wilson, E. O. (1984). The biophilia hypothesis. Harvard University Press.

Wymelenberg, K. (2014, March 19). The benefits of natural light. Archlighting.com.

Zeiler, W. (2011). Overview from passive house schools and NZEB schools to plus energy schools. Architecture and Sustainable Development 27th Annual International Conference on Passive and Low Energy Architecture. Proceedings; Volume 2

Zelinka, A., & Harden, S. (2005). Placemaking on a budget: improving small towns, neighborhoods, and downtowns without spending a lot of money. American Planning Association.

VIOLENCE

Austen, (2022, March 28). How Thousands of Indigenous Children Vanished in Canada. The New York Times.

Alan, S. (2015). Journalism and the culture of othering. Brazilian Journalism Research, 10 (2), 188–203

Alberta Council of Women's Shelters. (2023). Indigenous women in Indigenous societies. Alberta Council of Women's Shelters.

Altaras, C., Penner, C. (Eds.). (2022). Resistance: Confronting violence, power, and abuse within peace churches. Institute of Mennonite Studies.

Anastasiou, H. (2023). The war on terror and terror of war: Bellicose nationalism versus peace and democracy. Lexington.

Azar, E. (1985). Protracted international conflicts: Ten propositions. International Interactions, 12(1), 59-70.

BBC. (2022, December 12). Winnipeg murders: Families of murdered indigenous women call for landfill search. British Broadcasting Company.

Blanchard, J. (2023). Living through the Great Depression. The Winnipeg Foundation.

Bleiweis, R., Boesch, D., & Cawthorne Gains, A. (2020). The Basic Facts About Women in Poverty. Center for American Progress.

Bombay, A., Matheson, K., & Anisman, H. (2014). The intergenerational effects of Indian Residential Schools:

Implications for the concept of historical trauma. Transcultural Psychiatry, 52 (3), 320-338.

Bonikowski, B. (2016). Nationalism in settled times. Annual Review of Sociology, 427-449.

Boudreau, T. (2011). When the killing begins: An epistemic inquiry into violent human conflict, contested truths, and multiplex methodology. In T. Matyok, S. Byrne, & J. Senehi (Eds.), Critical issues in peace and conflict studies (pp. 19-42). Lexington Books.

Brandon, J. (2022). The Winnipeg street census: Final report. Winnipeg: End Homelessness and Social Planning Council of Winnipeg.

Bussidor, I., Bilgen-Reinart, U. (2000). Night spirits: The story of the relocation of the Sayisi Dene. University of Manitoba Press.

Butt, D. (2013). Colonialism and postcolonialism. The International Encyclopedia of Ethics.

Byrne, S., & Senehi, J. (2012). Violence; analysis, intervention and prevention. Ohio University Press.

Canada. (2014). Mood and anxiety disorders. Canada.ca.

Canada. (2019). Reclaiming power and place: The final report of the national inquiry into missing and murdered Indigenous women and girls. Volume 1a. Government of Canada.

Canada. (2019). Reclaiming power and place: The final report of the national inquiry into missing and murdered Indigenous women and girls. Volume 1b. Government of Canada.

CBC. (2009, June 16). Human Rights Museum mistreating First Nations heritage: archeologist. Canadian Broadcasting Company.

Cecco, L. (2023, April 5). Horror in Winnipeg as another Indigenous woman's body found in landfill: 'It keeps happening'. The Guardian.

Chandler, D. (2006). Empire in denial; The politics of statebuilding. Pluto.

Charron, A. (2022). Indigeneity, displacement, and regional place attachment among IDPS from Crimea. Geographical Review, 112 (1), 86-102.

Chomsky, N. (1977, May). The passion for free markets. Z Magazine.

Chrismas, B., & Chrismas, B. (2021). Modern-day slavery, human rights, and the sex industry. Journal of Community Safety and Well-Being, 6, 179-183.

Cook, L., Logan, T., & Parmen, J. (2018). Rural segregation and racial violence; Historical effects of spatial racism. American Journal of Economic Sociology (pp. 821-847).

Crossman, A. (2013). Labeling theory. About Education.

Desmond, M. (2023). Poverty, by America. Crown.

Durkheim, E. (1933). The division of labor in society. MacMillan Company.

Dutchen, S. (Spring 2021). The effects of noise on health. Noise pollution is more than a nuisance, it's a health risk. Harvard Medical School. Harvard Medicine.

Galtung, J. (1990). Cultural violence. Peace Research, 17(3), 291–305.

Greenstein, R., Sabatini, F., & Smolka, M. (2000). Urban spatial segregation; Forces, consequences, and policy responses. Lincoln Institute of Land Policy.

Hanson, E. (2009). Sixties scoop. University of British Columbia; Indigenous Foundations.

Hardy, K., & Laszloffy, T. (2005). Teens who hurt. Guilford Press.

Hill, E., Tiefenthaler, A., Triebert, C., Jordan, D., Willis, H., & Stein, R. (2020, May 31). How George Floyd Was Killed in Police Custody. The New York Times.

History. (2017). Mexican American War. A & E Television Networks. https://www.history.com/topics/19th-century/mexican-american-war

Horowitz, J., Igielnik, R., & Kochnar, R. (2020, January 9). Trends in income and wealth inequality. Pew Research Center.

Howes, M. (2017). Environmental sustainability: A case of policy implementation failure? MDPI.

Hutchison, P. Nyks, K., & Scott, J. (2017). Requiem for the American dream. Youtube.

Jackson, M. (2009). Neo-colonialism, same old racism: A critical analysis of the United States' shift toward colorblindness as a tool for the protection of the American colonial empire and white supremacy. Berkeley Journal of African-American Law & Policy, 11(1), 10, 156-192.

Jafari, M., Khosrowabadi, R., Khodakarim, S., &

Mohammadian, F. (2019). The effect of noise exposure on cognitive performance and brain activity patterns. National Library of Medicine, 2924–2931.

Kendi, I.X. (2016). Stamped from the beginning; the definitive history of racist ideas in America. Bold Type Books.

Krugman, P. (2012, May 3). Plutocracy, paralysis, perplexity. The New York Times.

Kuo, R., & Marwick, A. (2021). Critical disinformation studies: History, power, and politics. Harvard Kennedy School Misinformation Review, 2(4), 1-12.

LA2050. (2023). Income inequality. LA2050.org.

Lang, R. (2000, October). Office sprawl: the evolving geography of business. Center on Urban & Metropolitan Policy. Fannie Mae Foundation.

Lansley, S. (2012). Inequality, the crash and the ongoing crisis. The Political Quarterly. 83(4), 754-761.

Lee, B. (2019). Structural violence. Wiley Online Library.

Limmena, M. (2021, July 26) How intergenerational trauma affects Indigenous communities. Science Borealis.

Malone, K. (2016, August 15). Manitoba's Sayisi Dene: Forced relocation, racism, survival. CBC News.

Medhurst, M., Ivie, R., & Scott, R. (1997). Cold war rhetoric; Strategy, metaphor, and ideology. Michigan State Univeristy Press.

Metcalf, S. (2017, August 18). Neoliberalism: the idea that swallowed the world. The Guardian.

Miller Center. (2023). McCarthyism and the Red Scare. University of Virginia Miller Center.

Mishel, L., Gould, E., & Bivens, J. (2015, January 6). Wage stagnation in nine charts. Economic Policy Institute.

Morales, A., Dong, X., Bar-Yam, Y., & Pentland, A. (2019). Segregation and polarization in urban areas. Royal Society Open Science.

Mostagir, M. (2020). Social inequality and the spread of misinformation. DeepBlue.

Murphy, E. K. (2014). Environmental noise pollution; Noise mapping, public health, and policy. Elsevier.

Muste, A. (1967, November 16). Debasing dissent. New York Times. New York Times.

Ontario Association of Food Banks. (2014). Hunger report. Ontario Association of Food Banks.

Pazzanese, C. (2016, February 8). The costs of inequality: Increasingly, it's the rich and the rest. The Harvard Gazette.

Peters, E. (2017, April 4). Rooster Town. The Canadian Encyclopedia.

Coté, S., & Keltner, D. (2012). Higher social class predicts increased unethical behavior. Proceedings of the National Academy of Sciences of the United States of America.

Porter, C. A. (2020, August 6). 'Racism Is pervasive and systemic' at Canada's Museum of Human Rights, report says . The New York Times.

Porter, C., & Austen, I. (1965). "Scarcity" in economic theory and policy . Social Science, 40(1), 22-30.

Prothrow-Stith, D., & Spivak, H. (2004). Murder is no accident. Jossey-Bass.

Pyke, A. (2016, March 21). Top infrastructure official explains how America used highways to destroy black neighborhoods. Think Progress.

Province of Quebec. (2023). Effects of environmental noise on physical health.

Rigolon, A., Browning, M., & Jennings, V. (2018). Inequities in quality of urban park systems: an environmental justice investigation of cities in the United States. Landscape and Urban Planning, 51-79.

Sachs, J. (2011, February 28,). Need versus greed. Project Syndicate.

Sahlins, M. G. (2017). Stone age economics. Routledge.

Sapolsky, R. (2015). Stress and the brain: individual variability and the inverted-U. Nature Neuroscience, 1344–1346.

Selwyn, B., & Leyden, D. (2022). Oligopoly-driven development: The World Bank's trading for development in the age of global value chains in perspective. Competition and Change 26(2), 174-196.

Sides, J., Tausanovitch, C., & Vavreck, L. (2022). The bitter end: The 2020 presidential campaign and the challenge to American democracy. Princeton University Press.

Silva, N. (2004). Aloha betrayed: Native Hawaiian

resistance to American colonialism. Duke University Press.

Sisson, P. (March 6, 2020). Expanding highways and building more roads actually makes traffic worse. Curbed. https://archive.curbed.com/2020/3/6/21166655/highway-traffic-congestion-induced-demand

Smith, C. (2012, October 2). A brief examination of neoliberalism and its consequences. The Society Pages.

Toews, O. (2018). Stolen city; Racial capitalism and the making of Winnipeg. Abeiter Ring Publishing.

Truth and Reconciliation Commission. (2014). Residential Schools. TRC 2014.

Tsembris, S. (2007). Measuring homelessness and residential stability: The residential time-line follow-back inventory. Journal of Community Psychology.

Turner, M., & Greene, S. (2023). Causes and consequences of separate and unequal neighborhoods. Urban Institute.

UIA. (2023). Inadequate infrastructure. The Encylopedia of World Problems & Human Potential.

UIA. (2023). Inhumane architecture. The Encyclopedia of World Problems & Human Potential.

Wade, L. (2016, December 26). Why is Nationalism Dangerous? The Society Pages.

Walters, J., & Westman, J. (1981). Noise and stress: A comprehensive approach. Environmental Health Perspectives, 41, 291-309.

Wiebe, J. (2022). Reassessing Mennonite environmentalism through settler-colonialism: Political deficiencies, historical omissions, and Indigenous responses. Mennonite Quarterly Review, XCVI (3).

Wilkinson, I. (2020). Caste; the origins of our discontents. Random House Publishing.

Wilkinson, R., & Pickett, K. (2010). The spirit level; Why greater equality makes societies stronger. Bloomsbury.

Winnipeg Regional Health Authority. (2017). Income inequality & health. Winnipeg: Winnipeg Regional Health Authority.

World Bank Institute. (2005, August 8). Introduction to poverty analysis. Poverty Manual.

Zon, H. V. (2013, February). The unholy alliance of neoliberalism and postmodernism. Poltieke Filosofie.

About the Author

Dr. Preston Lindsay is a peacebuilder, scholar, and practitioner specializing in positive peace, infrastructures and cultures of peace, and spatial peace. He holds a PhD in Peace and Conflict Studies, where his research focused on measuring positive peace and translating peace theory into tangible, community-level impact.

His work bridges academic research and real-world application, helping communities understand how peace is shaped not only by policy and politics, but also by the environments we inhabit, the relationships we cultivate, and the ways we listen to one another.

Cultures of Peace is an initiative of **Born Brown : Institute**, a non-profit organization whose mission is to amplify and activate meaningful conversations for political and social awakenings. Driven by the approach of peacebuilding through kinship, Cultures of Peace works to break the cycles of disconnection, polarization, and apathy. Its mission is to create cultures and infrastructures of positive peace that nurture connected kinship, deep trust, and are self-determined through integrated strategies. BornBrown.us | CulturesOfPeace.us